*Cong*

You have just purchas...
and Feng Shui pers...

You've made a great i...
love the specialized in...
love, business, wealth and career in 2010!

But wait! Don't' Stop Here... There's More!

Now you can discover other powerful feng shui secrets
from Lillian Too that go hand-in-hand with the valuable
information you will find in this book.

And it's ABSOLUTELY FREE!

## LILLIAN TOO's
## NEW Online Weekly Ezine FREE!

You've taken the first step by purchasing this book. Now
expand your wealth, luck and knowledge and sign up
immediately! Just go to www.lilliantoomandalaezine.com
and register today!

It's EASY!  It's FREE!  It's FRESH & NEW!

Don't Miss Out!  Be one of the first to register at
www.lilliantoomandalaezine.com

Lillian's NEW Online FREE Weekly Ezine is only
available to those who register online at
www.lilliantoomandalaezine.com

# LILLIAN TOO &
# JENNIFER TOO

## FORTUNE & FENG SHUI

# Boar

# 2010

**Fortune & Feng Shui 2010 BOAR**
by Lillian Too and Jennifer Too
© 2010 Konsep Lagenda Sdn Bhd

Text © 2010 Lillian Too and Jennifer Too
Design and illustrations © Konsep Lagenda Sdn Bhd

The moral right of the authors to be identified as authors of this book
has been asserted.

Published by KONSEP LAGENDA SDN BHD (223 855)
No 11A, Lorong Taman Pantai 7, Pantai Hills
59100 Kuala Lumpur, Malaysia

For more Konsep books, go to www.konsepbooks.com
or www.lillian-too.com
To report errors, please send a note to errors@konsepbooks.com
For general feedback, email feedback@konsepbooks.com

ISBN 978-967-329--037-6
Published in Malaysia, July 2009

for more on all the recommended
feng shui cures, remedies & enhancers for

2010
please log on to

www.wofs.com/2010

and

www.fsmegamall.com

# YEARS OF THE BOAR

| Birth Year | Western Calendar Dates | Age | Kua Number Males | Kua Number Females |
|---|---|---|---|---|
| Wood Boar | 4 Feb 1935 – 23 Jan 1936 | 75 | 2 West Group | 4 East Group |
| Fire Boar | 22 Jan 1947 – 9 Feb 1948 | 63 | 8 West Group | 7 West Group |
| Earth Boar | 8 Feb 1959 - 27 Jan 1960 | 51 | 5 West Group | 1 East Group |
| Metal Boar | 27 Jan 1971 – 14 Feb 1972 | 39 | 2 West Group | 4 East Group |
| Water Boar | 13 Feb 1983 – 1 Feb 1984 | 27 | 8 West Group | 7 West Group |
| Wood Boar | 31 Jan 1995 – 18 Feb 1996 | 15 | 5 West Group | 1 East Group |
| Fire Boar | 18 Feb 2007 – 6 Feb 2008 | 3 | 2 West Group | 4 East Group |

You are a BOAR born if your birthday falls between the above dates

# Contents

OVERVIEW - TIGER YEAR 2010                                      10

BOAR'S HOROSCOPE IN 2010
Part 1. Outlook & Luck for the Year                             42

Part 2. Compatibility with Others
- Boar With Rat – Water energy works in their favor            84
- Boar With Ox – Cannot find common ground                    86
- Boar With Tiger – Secret friends with Ho Tu                  88
- Boar With Rabbit – Boar brings good fortune                 90
- Boar With Dragon – Dragon finds an unlikely friend          92
- Boar With Snake – Enmity surfaces strongly                  94
- Boar With Horse – Solid and dependable pair                 96
- Boar With Sheep – Romance & comfort with your ally          98
- Boar With Monkey – Must try to stay true                    100
- Boar With Rooster – Very strongly benefiting the Boar       102
- Boar With Dog – Making the most of the Tiger year           104
- Boar With Boar – Being a lot more pleasant                  106

Part 3. Monthly Horoscopes
- February 2010 – Low level of tolerance this month           109
- March 2010 – Health luck low; young children be careful     112
- April 2010 – Excellent growth opportunities this month      115
- May 2010 – Success luck gets magnified                      118
- June 2010 – Income increases; prosperity luck              121
- July 2010 – Do not change jobs or employ new people        124
- August 2010 – Someone powerful comes to your aid           127
- Sept 2010 – Minor argument escalates into big fight        130

- October 2010 – Romance blossoms ... 133
- November 2010 – Luck soars but you are on a short fuse ... 136
- December 2010 – Watch what you eat; sleep early ... 139
- January 2011 – Good time to plan ... 142

# Part 4. Updating your House Feng Shui

- Yearly Feng Shui Afflictions ... 148
- Luck of Different Parts of Home ... 151
- Activating Good Star Numbers ... 154
- Luck Stars of the 24 Mountains ... 159
- Illness Star 2 Hits the NE in 2010 ... 160
- Ligitation Star 3 Hits the South in 2010 ... 163
- Misfortune Star 5 Hits the SW in 2010 ... 166
- Robbery Star 7 Strikes the SE in 2010 ... 175
- The Tai Sui Resides in the NE in 2010 ... 178
- The Three Killings Flies to the North in 2010 ... 181
- The Lucky 4 Star Brings Romance & Study Luck to the North ... 184
- White Star 1 Brings Triumphant Success to the West ... 188
- Celestial Star 6 Creates Windfall Luck in the East in 2010 ... 190
- Updating Your Feng Shui ... 193

# Part 5. Boar's Personal Feng Shui Luck

- Finetuning Your Personal Directions ... 196
- To Activate Success Luck ... 201
- To Maintain Good Health ... 209
- Becoming a Star at School ... 211
- Attracting Romance ... 213
- Interacting with the Annual Lo Shu Number 8 ... 215
- Safeguarding Boar's Afflicted Direction in 2010 ... 220
- Improving Your Door Feng Shui ... 221
- Special Talismans for the Boar ... 225

# OVERVIEW - TIGER YEAR 2010

The Golden Tiger Year of 2010 reflects the character of the Tiger – an aggressive, fierce and tough year that is also resilient and with hidden good fortune possibilities. This year is one of discordant energies. There are obstacles and frustrations ahead due to clashing elements and the aggressive nature of the Tiger year makes things appear worse than they actually are.

We face a scenario lacking in good signs; several indicators suggest a challenging year. For many animal signs, 2010 is a time of tough choices and hard circumstances.

For the Boar, the Tiger brings mixed signals, but the all-important Life Force of this sign is average, neither good nor bad. As with all the other twelve signs, Water Boars enjoy the best luck indications and this 27 year old has both financial and success luck. Other Boars have totally neutral readings for their chi energy levels and for their Life Force.

The Golden Tiger year does not bring smooth sailing to everyone; only those who stay resilient can successfully transform the year's problems into opportunities. It is vital not to get mentally defeated by the year's fierce energy and feng shui afflictions. The Boar must dig deep to find your inner strength. At the same time, you should make a real effort to study how the year's afflictions can be defeated, and then systematically apply remedies to the misfortune sectors. This will bring beneficial energy flowing to your NW location.

> **Tiger Years bring out the best in many people. Forced to overcome strenuous situations, many will rise to the challenge. For those born in the year of the Boar, it is likely that the stronger willed amongst you who are able to think positively and transcend the ferocity of the Tiger Year will be able to rise above the bad chi and thrive. You must think positive and be mentally strong in the face of challenges.**

The coming 12 months from February 4th 2010 to February 4th 2011 will test the most resilient of professionals and the most positive amongst us. The Year of the Ox just passed has been relatively stable but nevertheless fragile. The Year of the Tiger is less stable, and conditions for work and business will be more difficult. This is a year when the elements clash directly - the **Metal** of the year's heavenly stem destroys the Tiger's intrinsic **Wood**. Superficially, this is not a good sign. Yet Metal, when used with skill and under special circumstances can transform Wood into something of great value. So even as Metal destroys Wood, it can transform Wood into an object of value. This is the hidden worth which all should strive to capture.

铁 *metal* — **destroys** → 木 *wood*

Natural luck is in short supply. But this does not mean we cannot create our own luck! The year's outlook simply manifests the way the elements of the year have arranged themselves as revealed in the Paht Chee chart, and in the Flying Star charts of 2010. These charts have proved accurate in past years and are worth analyzing.

**With the elements of the year clashing, hostilities can get uglier, competition nastier and the environment itself more hostile. Heaven and Earth energy are not in sync. It is left to mankind to use our creativity and prowess to rise to the year's challenges and emerge triumphant.**

Note however that while the elements of the year influence the way luck manifests on a macro level, it is at the micro levels that an individual's luck is determined; and your elements at the micro level can be enhanced or subdued, can be transformed and made better. Here is where understanding astrological indications and feng shui can be so helpful.

There are ways to overcome negative energies caused by a clash of elements brought by missing elements, made worse by visiting "stars" of the 24 mountains or affected by elements hidden in the paht chee chart of the year. The "afflictions" we have to confront in the Year of the Tiger, or in any year, can all be remedied.

## Remedial Actions

We can create elements that are missing, replenish those that are in short supply, subdue misfortune stars and strongly activate the positive stars that bring good fortune to any home. This is the feng shui aspect of corrective work that can be done to improve the prosperity potential of your home.

The luck of individuals can also be improved by using element astrology and this is laid out in detail in the section on Annual Element Horoscopes which explains how the different elements of the Tiger Year affects you based on your animal sign of the Boar and also the element of your heavenly stem at birth. You can examine the pluses and minuses of your horoscopes to improve your luck for the year. You can use our suggestions and take steps to minimize whatever horoscope obstacles afflict your sign. This year we also offer suggested remedies.

Determine the elements that are missing or weak in your birth horoscope. Note what element requires replenishment. Take note of particular afflictions that can cause you the most problems. Then subdue them. Your animal sign scenario and outlook changes from year to year, so it is important to update.

## Four Pillars Ruling the Year
### Overweight Wood

The year's ruling four pillars chart shows there is an excess of Wood element, led by the Tiger whose intrinsic element is Yang Wood. Tiger appears twice, in the Year and in the Month Pillars, making its influence and that of the Wood element very strong. Note also that another Yin Wood is brought by the Rabbit. So there are three **Wood branches** in the chart.

These are supplemented by yet another Wood, i.e. the Yin Wood stem of the Day Pillar, making a total appearance of **four Wood elements in the chart.** The

| PAHT CHEE CHART 2010 - YEAR OF THE GOLDEN TIGER | | | |
|---|---|---|---|
| **HOUR** | **DAY** | **MONTH** | **YEAR** |
| HEAVENLY STEM<br>己<br>YIN EARTH | HEAVENLY STEM<br>乙<br>YIN WOOD | HEAVENLY STEM<br>戊<br>YANG EARTH | HEAVENLY STEM<br>庚<br>YANG METAL |
| EARTHLY BRANCH<br>乙卯<br>RABBIT WOOD | EARTHLY BRANCH<br>辛酉<br>ROOSTER METAL | EARTHLY BRANCH<br>甲寅<br>TIGER WOOD | EARTHLY BRANCH<br>甲寅<br>TIGER WOOD |
| HIDDEN HEAVENLY STEMS OF THE YEAR | | | |
| YIN WOOD | YIN METAL | YANG EARTH<br>YANG WOOD<br>YANG FIRE | YANG EARTH<br>YANG WOOD<br>YANG FIRE |
| The year is desperately short of WATER | | | |

intrinsic element of the year is therefore **Strong Yin Wood.** This excess of the Wood element suggests a year fraught with competitive pressures, when even friends can become devious in the interests of surviving through a tough time. But the Wood element will get depleted.

Two Earth elements symbolically distract Wood, and two Metal elements symbolically destroy Wood. This would have been fine if the Wood was being renewed by the presence of Water. The chart however is missing Water and missing Fire. The Wood of the year thus signifies dead and dying wood that cannot grow. With crucial elements missing, expansion and productivity is greatly strained this year. The work scenario is tough!

## Unbalanced Chart

With two elements missing and with too much Wood, the chart is considered unbalanced. This is not an auspicious sign. The presence of both yin and yang pillars makes up for this imbalance to some extent as neither positive yang nor negative yin energies dominate.

**Two Metal** in the chart suggests that power and rank come into focus during the year. There is no lack of leadership or mentor luck, and there is both yang as well as yin metal, male and female. Powerful men and women play a big role in the promise of the year's outlook.

**Two Earth elements** in the chart signify the presence of wealth luck. There is more wealth luck this year than last year. So despite an imbalance of elements in the chart, prosperity luck is present. This means there are **opportunities for making money** during the year.

What is needed to actualize wealth luck in 2010 is Water. It is only when the year's Wood element can flourish, grow and bring itself to fruition that money can be made. Wood needs Water, which is missing; WATER must thus be created!

The missing Water is significant. In addition, Fire is also missing. Without Water there can be no growth luck, and without Fire, there is no creativity! In the chart, the Fire element symbolizes ingenuity, intelligence, strategic thinking and mental clarity. Without clear foresight and creativity, the year lacks the spark to get things moving.

Those wishing to succeed must generate the Fire element within their living space, or personify this element by wearing the shades of the Fire element – red. Only then will you be resourceful enough to forge ahead. What is needed in the Year of the Tiger is vision and imagination. If you can think of original ways of moving ahead in your career or in your work, you will benefit greatly.

# Hidden Elements

Since the year suffers from missing elements, we next examine if there are any hidden elements in the chart. Usually earthly branches always have hidden heavenly stems and in 2010, the three animals of the year; i.e. the Tiger, Rooster and Rabbit do bring additional elements that supplement the year's luck further. The Tiger hides yang Earth, yang Wood and Yang Fire in the chart, and since Tiger appears twice in the chart, there are **two hidden Yang Fire.**

This suggests hidden creativity, resourcefulness and ingenuity as a result of which the year benefits. This is a good sign. And since Fire exhausts Wood, its hidden presence will also subdue competitive pressures.

**However, there is no sign of hidden Water!**

This serious lack of water means that although the essence of the year is strong wood, missing Water suggests rotting and depleting wood. It is hard to accumulate asset wealth in 2010. Those of you who create a powerful water feature in your work or living space are certain to benefit. Water is what brings excellent feng shui to the year 2010! Note that it is the 27 year old Water Boar who this year enjoys the best financial luck of all the Boars!

# Crouching Tiger Hidden Dragon

A significant observation of the 2010 paht chee chart is the presence of the **Rabbit** which belongs to the Wood element, same as the Tiger. The two animals are symbols of Spring, and when combined with the **Dragon,** a trinity of animal signs get created that produce a very strong *Seasonal Combination of Spring.* These 3 animals rule the East and their combined strength is enormously empowering, especially as their presence is conducive to **creating auspicious new beginnings**!

The Paht Chee Chart of the year contains all the ingredients required to generate the auspicious presence of the Dragon. It is thus extremely auspicious to invite the Dragon image into your home in 2010.

The good news is that the Crouching Tiger can cause the Hidden Dragon to surface. This is the source of the well known descriptive phrase "Hidden Dragon, Crouching Tiger" made so famous some years ago by the Ang Lee directed movie of the same name. And since the Month Pillar of the year's chart has Yang Earth, this is the ingredient required for the Dragon to rise from the ground and to fly magnificently into the skies. If this energy can be simulated, the Dragon creates the precious auspicious breath that brings good luck.

It is thus significant that there is also the presence of Rooster in the chart, as the Rooster is the Dragon's secret friend! The Rooster symbolizes the Phoenix enticing the Dragon to make an appearance! The paht chee chart of the year possesses all the ingredients required to generate the auspicious presence of the Dragon! It is very auspicious to invite the Dragon image into your home.

For the Boar, placing the Dragon inside a water feature in the East will still benefit you enormously as it basically activates the seasonal combination of Spring for you; and it also activates the Water element simultaneously. This is the key to enjoying a good year.

The Dragon is the celestial creature that will bring great good fortune to the year 2010. So it is really beneficial to place a miniature waterfall which features the images of the crouching Tiger, the hidden Dragon and the Rabbit, in the East sector of the home.

In 2010, this direction is visited by the celestial heavenly star of 6 which brings good fortune. Placing Water in the East not only activates the luck of a good Spring, it also makes up for the lack of a lap chun caused by the lunar year starting late.

The key to creating good energy for 2010 is a Dragon/Tiger/Rabbit water feature in the East!

The wearing of any kind of precious or semi-precious earth stone or of any kind of **Dragon jewellery** is especially meaningful in 2010. The stone signifies Earth which brings wealth luck, while the Dragon activates the luck of new beginnings, transforming the year's Tiger energy to work powerfully in your favor. Remember that the Dragon can subdue the fierce Tiger and what is needed is the mentally charged energy to activate the chi energy! The presence of the Dragon image completes the seasonal trinity of Dragon/Tiger/Rabbit.

# Auspicious & Dangerous Stars

In 2010, two potentially auspicious stars and two potentially dangerous stars make an appearance. Both stars are powerful in their beneficial and malefic influences respectively. The two lucky stars bring good fortune; these impact different animal signs differently and in varying degrees but they are generally beneficial.

## 1. Mentor Star

In Chinese astrology, much is made of "mentor" luck, which in the old days was an important factor bringing career success, especially to those who are young and ambitious. This star is sure to benefit the **27 year old Water Boar** whose personal financial luck is strong in 2010. A powerful mentor entering your life at this time will help to strengthen your success luck and is enormously beneficial. The mentor can be a godparent, an elder cousin, a boss or an influential uncle or aunty.

Hang a picture of someone you respect in your NW corner to actualize a mentor into your life! Remember that success often

comes from "who you know rather than what you know." This star is also referred to as the **Heavenly Virtue Star**. With its presence in the chart of the year, it indicates that help comes from powerful people. To activate for this star to manifest successfully for you, use the **double six big smooth amulet** comprising 6 large coins laid out in a row.

## 2. Star of Prospects

This favorable star brings a special energy that rewards determination and staying power. Those who have a passion for success will benefit from its presence. There is nothing that cannot be achieved for those prepared to work smart. Here we see ambition playing a big role in making the best of what the year brings. To activate this star in your favor make sure you have a Rabbit/Dragon/Tiger spring combination in the East of your home. This advice is especially directed to the **51 year old Earth Boar** whose finance luck is average but for whom success luck is good, but health luck is negative. Using Water to activate this Star of Prospects will give strength to your health luck. This is what will help you attain bigger success.

The Star of Prospects brings success to those with determination and ambitions. It rewards those who are focused.

### 3. Star of Aggressive Sword

This star is brought by the Tiger and there being two Tigers, it suggests that the Aggressive Sword's negative effects comes with a double whammy. This star brings fierce, ruthless and violent chi energy. People will push ahead at the expense of others using fair means or foul. The name of this star is *Yang Ren*, which describes yang essence (as in yin or yang) sharp blade that inflicts damage. This star has great potential for good or bad influences to materialize during the year, but it is more negative than positive. The excess Wood in the year's chart makes things worse. To protect against falling victim to this star's aggressive influence, wear the **Double Ring Talisman**. Also excellent for overcoming the ferocity of the Aggressive Sword Star are the **Trinity Ring** and pendants signifying heaven, earth and mankind chi. These come with powerful mantras of the Lotus family of Buddhas – Amitabha, Chenrezig and Manjushuri.

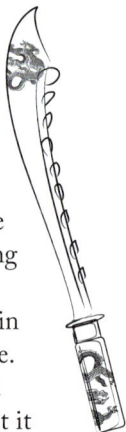

Wear the Trinity Ring with mantra to protect yourself against the Star of Aggressive Sword. This Trinity Ring also signifies the trinity of *tien ti ren* - which is very auspicious.

Finally, a third remedy is the **Fire Magic Wheel** for those who may be especially badly hit by the year's fierce Tiger energy. If you find yourself falling ill a lot or being hit by big doses of bad luck and disappointments, any one of these amulets are powerful ways to repel the bad luck.

Fire Magic Wheel

## 4. Star of External Flower of Romance

This is sometimes confused with the *peach blossom star* because it addresses the destiny of love. When the *flower of romance* is present in any year, it suggests love blossoms easily between people but it is not the kind of love that leads to marriage and family; it indicates instead the possibility of extramarital affairs bringing stress to happily married couples.

There is a difference between internal romance and external romance, and in the Year of the Tiger, it is the latter rather than the former that prevails. So the year will see increased occurrences of infidelity. In 2010, the Rabbit in the Hour Pillar is the Romance Star of the Tiger, and because Rabbit occurs in the

Hour Pillar, it signifies the *external romance star* and this makes all marriages vulnerable. Things are made worse by the Rooster in the Day Pillar, as Rooster clashes with Rabbit. This causes misunderstandings, although for the most part, infidelity in 2010 does not lead to divorce.

What all this means for the Boar is that there could be strains on your marriage caused by an outside love interest. It is wise not to over react when confronted with some hard truths either from your side or from that of your spouse.

## Feng Shui Chart of the Year

The destiny luck of the year is also influenced by the year's feng shui chart, which reveals lucky and unlucky sectors of buildings, houses and apartments. The chart comprises a 3 x 3 sector grid of numbers that reveals the luck distribution of the year. 2010's chart is explained in detail in Part 4 of this book.

The fortune-bringing stars of the 24 Mountains also affect the luck of the different sectors of your living space. These stars add important nuances to what is revealed in the annual chart, and their combined influences also affect the luck of each individual animal sign. There are 108 different Fortune Stars, but only a handful fly into each of the 24 Mountain directions in any year. These bring auspicious or harmful influences, but vary in strength and type each year.

Some stars bring good luck, some bring misfortune, while others bring protection. When your sign is negatively afflicted and your vitality gets weakened, you should wear specific protective Taoist charms. When your energy is heightened, the stars help you manifest whatever good fortune comes your way.

## Monthly Readings for the Whole Year

This book contains month to month readings of your luck to highlight the different chi energy of each month. They reveal significant high and low points of each month. The idea is to be alerted to auspicious as well as unlucky months.

**For the Boar, do note that the Hsia calendar months of Tiger (February), Rabbit (March) and Sheep (July) are months when allies and friends make the energies favorable.**

Nothing works better than to be prepared for sudden reversals of fortune, and in knowing when a particular misfortune can happen. When forewarned, you have enough time to put remedies into place and to wear cures to suppress the affliction. This is the best way of avoiding misfortune! Better to subdue bad luck than to wait for bad things to happen and then regret.

This is what motivates us to carefully research and analyze the Almanacs and source books to bring you accurate monthly readings that are an essential component of these books. Timely warnings are given in the monthly readings on Career, Business, Family, Love and Study luck.

These take account of each month's Lo Shu numbers, element, trigram and paht chee luck pillars. These are usually very accurate not just in identifying your good and bad months; they also offer valuable advice on when to lie low and when to move confidently forward. It will help you to get your timing right on important decisions and actions.

Our books on the 12 animal signs this year follow our tradition of bringing advice that is specific, focused and timely. The recommendations here are meant to alert you to months when you are vulnerable to illness, accidents or dangers. The good luck months are when significant opportunities come to you. Knowing *when* is certain to give you a competitive edge. This year we have added new dimensions that bring yet greater depth to our recommendations on timing.

# Feng Shui of your Living Space

A section is devoted to vital Feng Shui updates to be attended to at the start of each New Year. This explains transformational energy patterns that create new lucky and unlucky sectors in 2010. You can then make all the necessary adjustments to the feng shui of your home and work place. Remedial cures are always necessary to dissolve bad energy that bring misfortune, accidents, illness and other afflictions. All houses are affected by new energy patterns. You may have enjoyed good feng shui last year, but the pattern of chi will have changed in 2010.

An excellent example is the NW sector of the home which is the home location of the Boar. Last year this sector benefited from the victory star number 1 which brings success over the competition; in 2010 this year, it enjoys the star of future prosperity which also brings completion luck. So the kind of luck we enjoy or play host to each year changes, sometimes in terms of the type of good luck and other times, good luck can change to bad luck and vice versa.

Element therapy is very effective for neutralizing bad energy patterns such as the illness star and for strengthening the good sectors. This year, the **good luck star number 8** is in the center of the chart. This development indicates that the year strongly benefits those whose homes have an open plan concept that does not "lock up" this auspicious star number.

If you have a **toilet** or a **store room** in the center of the home, this can cause good luck to dissipate or stagnate; but if the center of your home is an **open space,** the good fortune chi flows seamlessly into the living areas of the home; and then 8 in the center brings extreme good fortune, more so when you install a **bright light** here. When the luck of 8 of the center is able to flow to other sectors, it particularly benefits the SW and the NE, as these are locations visited by the afflictive stars 2 and 5, two Earth numbers that transform into potential good fortune stars when they connect with the 8 to form the parent string combination of 2/5/8. Such a configuration which suppresses the negative aspect of 2 and 5 is only possible when there are no walls to block the energy of 8 from flowing outwards.

## Generating Wealth Luck in 2010

This is not going to be an easy year. For the Boar however, the year's energy looks very promising in terms of prosperity luck. There is wealth luck for the all those born in the Boar Year although what is coming is small wealth rather than big wealth. This is better than for many people, for whom wealth luck could well be elusive.

Also do note that any new wealth created will not be the kind of mega quick bucks generated through escalation of capital appreciation; instead wealth will be made in new areas of creative enterprise. Making money in 2010 will be a risky proposition because the year of the Tiger always holds risks. Riding the Tiger requires courage and nerves of steel!

So for the Boar, it is necessary to be careful especially if investing in shares and plunging back in to the markets. Better to postpone making any big decisions to the next year.

The world's economy is presently going through a major transformation; we are living through the Age of an Information Revolution where news/technology and ideas are accessible to everyone. New wealth comes less from traditional sectors and more from new creativity, technology, energy sources and ways of packaging. In short, from inventive product and service initiatives.

It is advisable to start the Tiger Year by being defensive. You will benefit from being protected so make very sure to place cures in all the afflicted sectors of your office and home. It makes sense to subdue the ferocious side of the Tiger. For those with dreams of making money who are prepared to take the risks, you can symbolically "Ride the Tiger" to activate its wealth-enhancing potential. Of all the twelve animal signs, the Boar is probably amongst the least commercially-minded! Those in business are strongly advised to enlist the aid of the Tiger subduing deities.

Most famous of the Taoist deities are the **Tiger-Taming Lohan**, the **Wealth God sitting on a Tiger**, and the **Immortal astride the Tiger.** Chinese legends contain tales of the wealth-bringing prowess of wise old Tiger, but this can only be unleashed when the wild side of this ferocious beast is adequately tamed!

Subduing the Tiger with his Magic Ring.

The Tiger Taming Lohan subdues the Year of the Tiger. This enables business people to make good from the year and tranform the Tiger's ferocity into wealth luck.

Place Tiger's open mouth looking outwards.

Hence in the Year of the Tiger, it benefits to invite in the three powerful deities who are close to the Tiger into your home. To many Chinese, they are the most powerful of Wealth Gods and their presence in any home or office attracts abundance.

**You can energize the Earth element for the center of the house to attract wealth luck and this is because Earth energy stands for wealth luck in 2010.**

To signify Earth, nothing works better than a **circular orb** rotating in the center of the home to attract wealth luck. A powerful wealth energizer for the home or any living or work area is to have a **solid rotating crystal ball** in the center. Those that come with an 8 embedded in gold in the center of the crystal ball are the best, although those who believe strongly in the power of mantras can also place the *Om Mani Padme Hum* rotating crystal ball here.

Last year we designed just such a crystal ball; we embossed the **21 Tara Praises** onto the crystal ball and these brought so much good fortune for us and everyone who used them. Rotating the crystal ball makes it very yang and that is what makes it generate fabulous energy. Shine a **light** on the crystal to empower it and to make it even more beautiful.

# Horoscope Luck of Elements

Staying lucky requires you to be personally empowered. The aura around you must be radiant and strong, not stagnant and weary. Hence being properly energized, healthy and staying astrologically strong are the three ingredients of attaining success luck in any year. What is important is to know exactly how your own personal elements interact with the elements of the year in 5 important categories.

Each of you, depending on your year of birth are born with different elements that affect the strength and quality of your **Life Force**; your **Inner Essence**; your **Success Potential**, the stability of your **Financial Luck** and the state of your **Health Luck**.

Your horoscope reveals the ruling elements that govern each of the 5 categories of luck, and how they interact with the 5 luck elements of the year. In 2010, the Life Force of the year is Wood, and its Spirit Essence is Water. Hence you can see that it is Water that strengthens Wood... it is the Spirit Essence that strengthens the Life Force of the year.

The year's Health Luck is governed also by Wood, while both the year's financial and success potential are governed by Metal. To find out how each person's birth elements interact with the luck elements of the year, we need to analyze how each person's element interacts with 2010's elements. This provides important information that enables you to enhance your potential enormously.

The analysis is based on your year of birth your heavenly stem and your earthly branch. Once you know how strong or how weak your horoscope elements are in 2010, you can easily dress, live and arrange your living space accordingly. This is discussed in detail for you in Part One of this book.

## The Power of Talismans

Protective talismans have the power to ward off misfortunes and each New Year it is incredibly important to know what talismans to wear and place in your home to ward off bad luck. In the Tiger Year, its imbalance of energy must be attended to if you want the year to be smooth for you.

Protective amulets possess added potency when made correctly. Circular discs and squares are excellent shapes to be used as amulets as these shapes are intrinsically powerful. Built-in Metal element energy of amulets made of steel or brass and with gold finish also have great power to suppress illness and misfortunes. The Chinese Almanac is an excellent source of talisman designs and good

Almanacs provide detailed images with invocations and explanations. These are older, rare editions which we have painstakingly compiled over the years as reference materials to ensure the amulets made comply with vital specifications. We have discovered that Tibetan-style talismans are very potent; these incorporate Sanskrit and Tibetan mantras which are really extremely powerful.

In the old days, Tibetan protection amulets were created by monasteries or very high lamas. These usually comprised mantras and images written onto paper and then folded to resemble mystical knots.

Traditional talismans are often covered with 5 colored cloth and tied with 5 colored string, which signify the 5 elements. Modern day amulets maintain the essence of the talismans but their quality of production is much better.

In terms of potency they are equally powerful, as modern technology has made it possible to have an incredible number of mantras inserted into the amulets!

# Tiger Year Talismans & Rituals

Here are some important amulets and rituals required for the coming year:

## Good Income Luck Talisman

Fashioned as a wealth vase, this amulet contains the *Taoist wealth fu* written on one side, with coins and ingots on the other side. This talisman is excellent to wear to protect against being laid off, losing one's source of income or to ensure that good business luck continues.

## The Tai Sui Amulet

This invokes the protection and goodwill of the Tai Sui who this year is once again a military general. This amulet carries a special Taoist invocation with a pair of Pi Yao images. The Boar is not directly affected by the Tai Sui, but it is still beneficial for you to carry the amulet which works by appeasing the Tai Sui.

Tai Sui Amulet

### Blue Water in a Globe

This Water element talisman is a potent way of making up for the lack of water in this year. Carrying this amulet everywhere you go symbolically brings growth luck. Water feeds the Wood energy of the year and this amulet is especially suitable for enhancing good wealth luck. For the Boar whose natural element is Water and whose element for success luck at birth is Fire, generating the presence of the Water element is what brings additional wealth luck. Water is in general short supply in 2010, hence everyone benefits from its physical presence. For the Boar, the presence of physical water ensures all other luck also materializes!

### The Double 6 Big Smooth Coins

This powerful good luck charm is suitable for the year 2010 as it invokes the Star of Powerful Mentors. The 6 large coins made of metal with gold finish ensure everything goes smoothly for you. Having it in your possession will bring you the influential help of someone powerful when you need it. Those in leadership or managerial positions benefit from carrying it.

## 5 Element Ringing Bell

The sound of metal hitting against metal creates the chi energy that can dissolve the power of the Five Yellow which in 2010 hurts the matriarch in all families. It is important not only to have this bell displayed in the SW corners of the home, but ringing the bell at least once a week magnifies its strength many times over.

Walk round each of your rooms in an anti-clockwise direction three times, all the while ringing the bell. This is an energy cleansing ritual which is safe and effective to use. It was not easy finding the kind of bells that produce the melodious sounds preferred for these bell amulets. But when you ring the bell you are instantly dissolving bad energy build up in your space. Do this ritual in rooms that are important to you.

**Boar** born people should undertake the bell ringing ritual on Saturdays of each week.

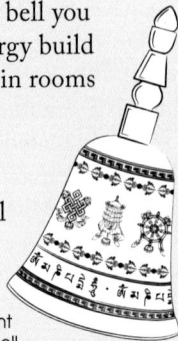

5-Element
Ringing Bell

## The Magic Fire Wheel Talisman

This is the Dharmachakra eight-spoked wheel surrounded by a circle of fire, indicating fire and gold energy. Inscribed in the circle is a very powerful mantra for subduing quarrelsome energy directed towards you. This talisman can effectively reduce gossip, slander, and office politics and even help you avoid court cases and legal entanglements. If you can consecrate these magic fire wheels, they are also effective protection against spirit harm.

## Precious Ring Talisman

This powerful talisman is said to possess magical powers. It is carried by the **Tiger Taming Arhat** who was a Brahmin named Pindola. Made of steel and plated with real gold, powerful Dharmakaya mantras can be inserted inside the ring. It should then be hung in the NE corner of your living room or office, or you can carry it with you as a bag hanging. The precious ring talisman is one of the most powerful ways of subduing the aggressive energy of a Tiger Year.

## The Double Circle Amulet

This wards off seriously troublesome chi energy brought by the combination of **Five Yellow** with the **illness star** afflictions. Wearing it as a pendant or hanging it in your animal sign direction is an effective way of overcoming the troublesome months where the configuration of star numbers brings combined danger of illness and misfortunes.

# Part 1
# Outlook for the Year 2010

- Wood Boar – 15 & 75 years
- Fire Boar – 63 years
- Earth Boar – 51 years
- Metal Boar – 39 years
- Water Boar – 27 years

Those born in the year of the Boar enjoy more than reasonable success luck. In 2010 they experience a vast improvement over the previous year's luck. There are a series of small but meaningful reasons to celebrate through the year, but don't expect earth-shattering success. For some of you suffering from afflicted feng shui, some heart stopping moments caused by falling victim to the robbery star might ensue. There are petty thieves clouding the year for you but by and large, this year's charts bring the chance to lay good groundwork for future prosperity.

The year is kind to you - the Tiger is your secret friend, so the Tiger Year is supportive. It promises to be productive in terms of making advancements. Some of you also enjoy excellent money luck, in particular the 27 year old Water Boar. The 63 year old Fire Boar will likewise have good money luck. For both, this year will be very pleasant indeed.

But for everyone born in a Boar year, the indications for Life Force luck and inner chi essence show only average readings. You can be somewhat lacking in vigor and spiritual strength. In fact there isn't sufficient vitality to make this into a spectacular year. The good news is that you can make up for this by placing greater emphasis on improving your attitude; making it really come alive with optimism. This year determination benefits!

## The Boar Personality in 2010

There is everything nice about the Boar personality. Thoughtful, sensitive and always super friendly, you continue to be this way in 2010. Your popularity is quite undiminished in the Year of the Tiger and for some of you even, the year enhances your glimmer and you could see an increase in your popularity. Despite only a mediocre showing in the energy and chi stakes, you somehow still manage to be come across lively and delightful to be with.

In 2010 the Boar turns on the charm. And while you are not normally a superficial, flighty sort of person, you will be quite happy this year to resonate with others mainly on surface levels.

You are not keen to go too deep with anyone, preferring to leave your inner most thoughts to yourself. So this year sees the Boar preferring to be secretive and unwilling to get into serious discussions on the whys and the wherefores of events or developments.

The work place is pleasant enough but Boars do have to contend with people who do not see eye to eye with you. So especially at work, the Boar will stay lowkey, skimming surface levels and resisting efforts from others to develop closer relationships.

In 2010, the Boar personality is detached and some would say even reserved. Even to those close to you, there is a reluctance to confide your inner thoughts. There is a tendency towards being more contemplative than ever.

Your interest in material success is still around but somehow this is no longer that important to you so although those of you belonging to the Earth Boar years and Metal Boar years whose financial luck is not great, this will not really get you down too much.

You will continue working of course but there is no great burning ambition to save the world or make a million dollars. Commercialised aspects of life do not hold out great attraction for you. Nor are you the type to hanker after fame or stardom. The Boar is happiest doing its own thing in 2010, and if this means being a loner, that is what you will tend towards.

Despite this, Boars remain excellent friends and are trustworthy individuals for those who come in close contact with them. The **27 year old Water Boar** will enjoy a year of great wealth luck and there is also a delightful absence of hindrances to success so efforts pay off and whatever you pursue is certain to actualise for you. Health is also not bad.

For the **39 year old Metal Boar,** health and success luck is good, but financially, the year tends to be unstable. The 51 year old Earth Boar goes through a pretty average year, while the **63 year old Fire Boar** enjoys a good year. Just watch your health!

Overall however, the Boar should do quite well in 2010. Those pursuing spiritual pursuits could gain some amazing realizations.

# LADY BOAR

| Birth Year | Type of BOAR Lady | Lo Shu at Birth | Age | Luck Outlook in 2010 |
|---|---|---|---|---|
| 1935 | Wood Boar Lady | 2 | 75 | Success & good health luck |
| 1947 | Fire Boar Lady | 8 | 63 | Work and finances are stable |
| 1959 | Earth Boar Lady | 5 | 51 | Averagely successful year |
| 1971 | Metal Boar Lady | 2 | 39 | Low on finances but still fine |
| 1983 | Water Boar Lady | 8 | 27 | Great money & success luck |
| 1995 | Wood Boar Girl | 5 | 15 | A year of scholastic success |

The Lady Boar's mood and disposition improves hugely in the Year of the Tiger. Vitality returns to this generally amiable woman. Her personal chi seems to be in better sync with that of the year and color returns to her cheeks as fast as smiles return to her face.

She walks with a much lighter step this way, enjoying her popularity and the goodwill of friends and loved ones. Those with whom she felt alienated with return to play a role in her life once more. Friendship resumes with a vengeance and it seems that everything bad is forgotten. It is a good year for reconciliations.

There is a good deal of emotional baggage that needs to be worked through, but in this Year of the Tiger, the Boar woman is better focused and operates with improved clarity of purpose.

There is also structured organisation in the way you approach your work and respond to relationships. You will continue to rely on your instincts but there will also be a practical side to your impulses. You are more in tune with reality as your head comes down from the clouds.

Socially, this will turn out to be a good year for the Boar woman as gossip subsides and fair weather friends disappear from your horizon. However there are petty and small time "thieves" who will give you a hard time, so learn to ignore these inconsequential mischief makers. In any case, this is a good year to stay a little reserved and not get too close to new acquaintances.

The **75 year old Boar** will enjoy excellent good health while the **63 year old Fire Boar** goes through a year marked by financial and work stability. The **51 year old lady** has an average year although there is good luck at the work place while the 39 year old finds herself low on finances. The **27 year old** enjoys a great year with superlative prosperity luck. This Water Boar lady benefits hugely from her water element and finds that 2010 will bring a relatively memorable year.

# GENTLEMAN BOAR

| Birth Year | Type of BOAR Man | Lo Shu at Birth | Age | Luck Outlook in 2010 |
|---|---|---|---|---|
| 1935 | Wood Boar Man | 2 | 75 | Growing old gracefully is YOU! |
| 1947 | Fire Boar Man | 8 | 63 | Stability & success this year |
| 1959 | Earth Boar Man | 5 | 51 | Moving along smoothly |
| 1971 | Metal Boar Man | 2 | 39 | Small money woes but still fine |
| 1983 | Water Boar Man | 8 | 27 | A superlative year for you |
| 1995 | Wood Boar Man | 5 | 15 | Achievements come easily |

The Gentleman Boar has a relatively good year to look forward to, especially when compared with the year just passed. Energy levels are average, but for all for you, the year will be smooth and there are few hindrances at the work place and professionally. Whatever setbacks there are can be easily overcome, and for some of you, 2010 could even turn out to be a superlative year. This is especially possible for the

Water Boar and Fire Boar who both enjoy reasonably great money and success luck.

The Boar guy's resource and energy levels have improved over last year's and your mental state of mind is more relaxed. As a result, there is good vitality and vigor which brings color back into your world. Expectations become positive and good results through the year will greatly improve your confidence.

As a result, it becomes much easier to be more self assured and to leave whatever insecurities that had been plaguing you behind. For most Boars, the difference in energy makes a genuine difference in the way you approach your work and react to friends and colleagues.

You will be less tense in the way you do your work, but you will maintain a reserve that makes it difficult for many people to get too close to you or to read your inner thoughts. But your popularity nevertheless improves because your own personal auric field also improves.

The **75 year old Wood Boar** feels healthier and more alert than ever while **63 year old Fire Boar** feels greatly re energized by the vitality of the New Year.

For you the year brings good wealth and success luck although health is not great. The **51 year old Earth Boar guy** also enjoys success but money luck is only moderately stable. The **39 year old Boar gentleman** enjoys a good healthy year and also good financial luck; but it is the **27 year old Water Boar** who has it best of all. For you money and wealth luck is at its peak and there is also great success coming to you in 2010. This is brought for you by your Water element heavenly stem; water is in short supply in 2010.

# Personal Luck Horoscope in 2010

This section focuses on the Personal Luck Horoscope of the Boar in 2010 and the chart of horoscopes for each Boar person is determined by the heavenly stem element of your year of birth.

The Horoscope Chart shows how Boar's ruling luck Elements in the year birth interacts with the Elements of the year 2010. The horoscope deals with 5 types of luck with each type being affected differently each year. Each of the Boar's 5 birth elements interacts with those of 2010 and this interaction reveals whether the year brings strength or weakness to that particular type of luck.

It is important to examine what kind of luck combination your animal sign's element horoscope brings you each year. This is because the element signifying the 5 types of luck changes from year to year. The 5 categories of luck and their significance is explained as follows:

# First, Your Life Force...

The most important "luck" to examine first is the Life Force as this reveals whether there are any hidden dangers or threats to the life span. Danger to one's life comes in many different forms and it can come suddenly without any notice at all. Death can also come to perfectly healthy people through accidents or unexpected natural disaster.

Astrologers always tell their clients that the only thing we can all be sure of is that everyone has to face death someday, but that the only thing we are never sure of is when that time of death is. When the indication to the Life Force luck shows a double cross, it suggests a threat to the Life Force that is usually karmic.

The presence of a circle and a cross - OX or XO - indicates that you will need some kind of protection during the year although there will be not much danger to your life. Nevertheless, there is a likelihood of some nasty accident or event happening that can put your life in some kind of danger. When other indications are not negative however the circle overrides the X and this is the case with the Boar in 2010. As such, the Life Force indicates that it may be advisable to wear amulets but there is little cause for worry overall.

## Second, Your Health Luck...

This is an indication of your physical health during the year so that those of you with a double cross - XX - should watch out as it indicates there will be health disorders that upset work schedules and cause mental distress. It also indicates that you are vulnerable to food poisoning and to catching wind borne diseases. Even a single cross - X - is indicative of some kind of health disorder so it is advisable to take counter measures.

One way of overcoming a negative indication is to give yourself a nick name or better yet just ask your friends and loved ones to stop calling you by name for the year. It is believed that negativities related to bad health luck is born by the wind and if your animal sign is also afflicted by the either the illness star or the Five Yellow star of the feng shui chart, then you must make very sure to install the remedies suggested.

Those whose charts indicate a double circle - OO - will sail through the year totally undisturbed by any health issues or concerns and even if they are recovering from illness contracted in previous years will show signs of recovery.

Good health indications also mean a happy state of mind with few things causing disturbances to your mental state. It also suggests that your attitude is generally positive during the year so you will get along extremely well with colleagues, co workers and family members. The year progresses smoothly.

A single circle - O - suggests that you will have few health problems during the year. Those whose charts indicate a cross and a circle - XO or OX - should have little cause to worry as here the circle overrides the cross causing you few problems. The year should move along fairly smoothly unless your animal sign is hit by the illness star afflictions.

## Third, Your Finance Luck...

This reveals the stability of your finances during the coming year. In many ways, it reveals if you are going to be better off or worse off in the coming twelve months. When Astrologers examine the compatibility of a couple for marriage purposes, this type of luck is studied in great detail, especially in assessing how the Elements in a man's chart affects the woman's chart, as this is the luck that reveals whether the woman can cause the man's economic standing after marriage to improve as a result of the woman's influence.

If your chart reveals a double circle - OO - it suggests that you can gain substantial new wealth in 2010. This is what the Fire Boar has this year, so it indicates that your financial luck is good and your prosperity levels make good and steady progress. Your business and projects proceed smoothly adding to your fortune. Needless to say, when your chart indicates three circles - OOO - it means your

wealth luck is even more certain to materialise.
The **27 year old Water Boar** enjoys this wonderful
indication so your business is likely to prosper and
whatever expansion plans you may be planning are
sure to be successful.

An indication of crosses is a negative reading. The
more crosses there are, the greater the instability of
your finances. A double cross - XX - in the chart for
this type of luck suggests a great deal of instability
in your economic situation. Business dealings could
suddenly turn sour and profits could get hit by some
unexpected calamity. This afflicts the oldest Boar here
to whom money luck should not be too important.
To overcome the bad luck here, you are advised to
immediately donate to some good cause. Contributing
to a worthwhile charity is the best way to overcome
the effect of fluctuating financials. Another way is to
invite the God of Wealth into the house.

Buddhists also recommend praying to or at least
acknowledging the **White Dzambhala Wealth
Buddha** who sits on a dragon, carries the gem
spouting mongoose and is attended by four offering
goddesses. This is a powerful antidote to counter
unstable money luck. If you even have a single cross
- X - against your Finance Luck in your chart this
year as is the case with the **39 year old Boar**, you

should be extra careful with your money. Definitely you should not start a new business and you should not invest in new ventures. This is not a good year to be careless with your funds. It is better to be conservative. Those playing the stock market should especially take note of what your indication of wealth luck shows. A cross with a circle - OX or XO - indicates a fairly stable situation. It does not suggest any loss.

## Fourth, Your Success Luck...

This reveals your prospects at work and what the year holds for you in terms of bringing achievement and attainments. This is the luck you should keep track of if you are still in school or if you are working for a company or have just started a new job. In essence it also reveals your mental alertness and whether you can make the best of the year.

Obviously if the indication is three circles - OOO - or two circles - OO - it means you are sure to enjoy good success luck in your work. Your career will be like a shooting star and there are promotion opportunities opening up for you. You could also be made a new job offer which brings recognition of your abilities and a higher paycheque.

All Boar people enjoy the luck of two circles and this

is definitely a positive indication of success but here you will need to watch your attitude and to make sure that you do not get big headed causing good fortune to transform into misfortune.

## Fifth, Your Spirit Essence...

This reveals your personal cosmic strength during the year. It shows if you will encounter spiritual obstacles and if you do whether you will get severely hurt. According to the Astrology Manuals, there are afflictions that arise from inadvertently meeting up with harmful wandering spirits or not knowingly upsetting or angering some worldly ghosts.

Examples of this are like saying the wrong things at temples or holy places, unfortunately peeing in open environments without first asking permission and then inadvertently hitting a wandering spirit, or unintentionally hurting other worldly beings hiding inside boulders or old trees.

The Chinese have always advocated being careful about upsetting the natural order of things and while these may seem like superstitious beliefs, nevertheless negative results arising from spiritual affliction can sometimes be so severe it can take months, even years to recover. Some people get sick while others may lose one of their senses, or they simply go mad or are mentally agitated without a seeming cure…

These unfortunate happenings can happen to people whose Spirit Essence is low like when the indication is a double cross – XX. Then it suggests a high probability of such a misfortune happening during the year.

When the reading is a cross and a circle - XO or OX - it suggests a danger but it also means that somehow you will find away to be shielded from feeling any severe effect. When you receive this indication it is advisable to wear some kind of protective amulet to subdue the negativity and to be fully protected during the year. Spiritual amulets can be very powerful for ensuring your physical and spiritual safety during the year; and it also protects against harm from poor health, or wealth luck.

Wearing protective mantras on your body can protect you from spirit harm. This Om Mani pendant is suitable for all animal signs in 2010.

# PERSONAL LUCK
## 15 & 75 Year Old Wood Boar

| Type of Luck | Element at Birth affecting this Luck | Element in 2010 affecting this Luck | Luck Rating |
|---|---|---|---|
| Life Force | Water | Wood | OX |
| Health Luck | Fire | Wood | OOO |
| Finance Luck | Wood | Metal | XX |
| Success Luck | Fire | Metal | OO |
| Spirit Essence | Metal | Water | OX |

Element influences on the Wood Boar in 2010

The Wood Boar's Element Horoscope Chart is shown above and it indicates that its ruling luck elements at birth combine well with the elements of the year that influence its health and success luck. As such you will enjoy good health this year and there is also a smooth ride for those of you still working. For the young teenager this year should bring you success at school and at examinations. The elements interacting against your financial luck show a negative interaction so there appears to be some financial instability for you this year. And as for the two more important luck indications against your Life Force and Spirit Essence, this shows an improvement over the previous year.

The Wood Boar basically enjoys good health this year and this suggests that unlike the previous year there should not be cause for worry. Your chi levels are also showing good levels, so mentally you will tend to be more alert this year than last. Nevertheless, it is not a bad idea to still be careful considering your age. What could cause you to feel tense and worry will be your negative financial indications.

This double XX against your Finance Luck however should not be given too great a significance since at this age you are unlikely to be too active on the stock market or likely to lose much money. Do not spend too much time worrying as this could cause you to get on a downward spiral of depression which will turn the luck of your Life Force against you.

You can, if you so wish, wear amulets to protect against loss of wealth in 2010. A great way of doing this really is to invite in a **Wealth God sitting on a Tiger** so that your secret friend the Tiger brings you some safeguards against loss of wealth.

# 63 Year Old Fire Boar

| Type of Luck | Element at Birth affecting this Luck | Element in 2010 affecting this Luck | Luck Rating |
|---|---|---|---|
| Life Force | Water | Wood | OX |
| Health Luck | Earth | Wood | XX |
| Finance Luck | Fire | Metal | OO |
| Success Luck | Fire | Metal | OO |
| Spirit Essence | Metal | Water | OX |

Element influences on the Fire Boar in 2010

The Fire Boar's Element Horoscope Chart is shown above and it indicates that your ruling luck elements at birth combine very well with the elements that influence your financial and success luck. These show double circles which basically indicate a stable and solid showing against these two kinds of luck.

As a result you will enjoy a relatively good year when things move smoothly. There is good fortune to be found at the place of work and those in business are certain to do well. Those working professionally can see their career take a leap forward. The Tiger Year will become memorable for you especially as the Tiger and Boar are secret friends, so 2010 is likely to be a pleasant time indeed.

The Boar ruled by the Fire Element is a courageous individual and your strong determination will be put to great good use this year as fortune smiles on you. Your elements also show that in other areas of luck this is a year of great improvements for you. You will find yourself a lot more confident as both your Life Force and inner spirit essence show a great improvement over the previous year. This brings greater vitality to your demeanor adding greater zest in your quest for success.

The main thing that should concern you this year are the double XX against your Health Luck as this makes you vulnerable to catching bugs and getting food poisoning. You should make every effort to be careful and also protect the health feng shui of your house. Make sure for instance that you place a **wu lou** in metal in the NW which is your direction and in the NE where the illness star resides in 2010. Remember that when it comes to health issues, this can be get to be very depressing when you contract something serious. It is better to be careful and avoid getting sick.

# 51 Year Old Earth Boar

| Type of Luck | Element at Birth affecting this Luck | Element in 2010 affecting this Luck | Luck Rating |
|---|---|---|---|
| Life Force | Water | Wood | OX |
| Health Luck | Wood | Wood | X |
| Finance Luck | Earth | Metal | OX |
| Success Luck | Fire | Metal | OO |
| Spirit Essence | Metal | Water | OX |

Element influences on the Earth Boar in 2010

The Earth Boar's Element Horoscope Chart is shown above and it indicates that your ruling luck elements at birth combine very well with the element that influences your success luck which shows a double circle OO and this indicates that the year has few hindrances for you. The work place is also a pleasant place to be… but for your health luck, the indication of a single X is cause for some concern. You have to be careful not to catch the odd bug as this could cause your health to take a turn for the worse. The year 2010 brings a very average year to this 51 year old Boar although it is still a great deal better than the luck of the previous year. The chart indicates a monotonous year for your finances with little change over the past year. Nevertheless, it is not a great year to take risks with your money. Better to play safe than regret. In any case, the year itself is quite challenging in terms of opportunities for making money.

Thankfully however, the chi energy level of this Boar has improved considerably, as there is a XO against its Life Force and Spirit Essence and what this means is that the new year will see you more confident and self-assured.

The Earth Boar is a down-to-earth and responsible person to whom the well being of family and loved ones are important. No matter what else the year brings, you are sure to focus strongly on your finances, making sure that this stays stable through the year; and indeed you will have small successes, and you will be successful at laying the groundwork for your family's future.

There is success luck on the cards and since your have good impulses it is more than likely you will get many of your decisions right in this Year of the Tiger. To improve your financial luck, do create good karmic merit by donating to worthwhile causes.

# 39 Year Old Metal Boar

| Type of Luck | Element at Birth affecting this Luck | Element in 2010 affecting this Luck | Luck Rating |
|---|---|---|---|
| Life Force | Water | Wood | OX |
| Health Luck | Metal | Wood | OO |
| Finance Luck | Metal | Metal | X |
| Success Luck | Fire | Metal | OO |
| Spirit Essence | Metal | Water | OX |

Element influences on the Metal Boar in 2010

The Metal Boar's Element Horoscope Chart is shown above and it indicates that your ruling luck elements at birth combine very well with the element of the year that influences your success and health luck. These show a double circle OO which suggests that the year has few difficulties for you at work. In fact, it indicates a good year professionally and there could even be upward mobility for those working for large companies. For those of you in business, this suggests that the year will be good for those wanting to launch a new product, to move in a new direction or to expand. However it is necessary to also take note of the single X against your money luck. So those in business should understand that there is little near term money to be made this year. Prosperity luck in fact is showing a negative and this can even mean a loss situation facing you. Thus while there may be good success indications, it is important to also accept the fact that cash flow wise it is unlikely to be a good year. So do be careful. Try to conserve cash and do not invest impulsively.

You are a 39 year old in your prime professionally. There is the possibility of career advancement as well so in 2010, we find you very focused on work and on actualising your professional ambitions. Sure, money and financial improvements are important to you but you are also a proud Boar focused on achieving success and enhancing your reputation.

Making it to the top is important to you. While other Boars may be happy to stay low key, you are not averse to creating the actuality of attaining high profile success. In many ways, this is in fact far more important to you than making money. It is true to say that you are the highest achieving of the Boars and you are actually quite unbending when it comes to attaining your dreams for recognition. Happily for you, 2010 is your year from this perspective.

# 27 Year Old Water Boar

| Type of Luck | Element at Birth affecting this Luck | Element in 2010 affecting this Luck | Luck Rating |
|---|---|---|---|
| Life Force | Water | Wood | OX |
| Health Luck | Water | Wood | OX |
| Finance Luck | Water | Metal | OOO |
| Success Luck | Fire | Metal | OO |
| Spirit Essence | Metal | Water | OX |

Element influences on the Water Boar in 2010

The Water Boar's Element Horoscope Chart shown above suggests that you are the luckiest of the Boars. Your ruling luck elements at birth for wealth luck and success combine very well with the elements that rule these same types of luck in 2010, as a result of which you enjoy truly incredible Finance Luck as well as very good Success Luck. For the other kinds of luck, you have a balanced showing of circles and crosses. Thus this coming year predicts a great improvement over the previous year. Most important are the improvements in your Life Force and chi strength luck as these bring back a much improved vitality to your personality. This year there is enthusiasm and verve in the way you approach your work. Your self esteem also improves by leaps and bounds.

This brings a very good feeling helping you to attain a great deal this year. The Water element is also such an excellent bonus or maybe it is itself the cause of your much improved energy levels and sources. The year is desperately short of water so the presence of this element in your chart is auspicious.

Being a Water Boar, you will definitely find the good chi this year. As a result, your social life improves even as your professional life takes on added sparkle. Most noticeably you will find the energy to see you through anything that requires follow through and real effort. You will thus overcome your intrinsic Boar nature, which is to party and have a good time. You have never been especially comfortable cast into the role of a workaholic – it is simply not in your nature. But being young and vivacious, having fun for you can be serious business, so it is just as well that you are going through an exciting year. The good news is that irrespective of how you respond to the year's opportunities, money will continue to flow towards you. This Tiger Year is when things just cannot go far wrong.

# Part 2
# How Boar Gets On with Others

In Chinese Astrology, your animal sign creates a variety of influences on your life, most significant of which is how it affects the way you interact and get on with the people around you, your partner, your parents, children, siblings, relatives and friends.

Knowing the fundamentals of astrological compatibilities can help you to make your relationships more harmonious, uplifting and definitely less aggravating. You will understand your reactions to people, why you have a natural affinity with some and an instant aversion to others; why some people just annoy you for no reason and why you easily overlook the faults of some others.

It all boils down to the affinity groupings, the secret friends and ideal soul mate pairings of the Chinese Zodiac! The horoscope compatibility groupings influence how you respond to each of the other eleven signs and explain the special relationships that inherently exist between them.

However, there are annual variations to the level of compatibility amongst animal signs. Everyone's energies, mood, aspirations and tolerance levels change from year to year. People tend to be more or less tolerant, more or less magnanimous or selfish, more distracted or warm depending on how they fare during any year.

When things go smoothly, one is better disposed to others, and even between two animal signs who are naturally antagonistic, there can still good affinity, enough for two unlikely animal signs to enjoy one another to the extent of becoming temporary soulmates!

Likewise when one is being challenged by a non-stop set of problems, then the slightest provocation can lead to anger even between zodiac friends and allies. That is when friends can become temporary enemies! A falling out between horoscope allies is not impossible.

Hence compatibility between animal signs takes account of time frames. In this section, we look at how the Boar person relates to others according to specific compatibility groupings, and also how it interacts with the other animal signs in 2010.

## Compatibility Groupings
1. Alliance of Allies
2. Paired Soulmates
3. Secret Friends
4. Astrological Enemies
5. Peach Blossom Links
6. Seasonal Trinity

## 1. Alliance of Allies
There are four affinity groupings of animal signs that make up Alliances of Allies. Each alliance comprises three animal signs who are natural allies of the Horoscope. The three signs within any alliance have similar outlooks and share similar goals. Their attitudes and thought processes are alike, and their support of and compatibility with each other tends to be instant and natural.

When all three animal signs enjoy good fortune in any year, the alliance becomes strong and powerful that year. When there is a natural alliance within a family unit as amongst siblings, or between spouses and a child, the family tends to be very united. They give strength to one another, and when they prosper, good fortune gets multiplied. Families that have alliances of allies are usually extremely close knit. This is one of the secret indications of good fortune. As an alliance, they become a formidable force.

## Alliances of Allies

| Ally Groupings | Animals | Characteristics |
|---|---|---|
| Competitors | Rat, Dragon, Monkey | Competent, Tough, Resolute |
| Intellectuals | Ox, Snake, Rooster | Generous, Focused, Resilient |
| Enthusiastic | Dog, Tiger, Horse | Aggressive, Rebellious, Coy |
| Diplomatic | Boar, Sheep, Rabbit | Creative, Kind, Emotional |

Allies always get along. Any falling out is temporary. They trust and depend on each other and immediately close ranks should there be an external threat. Good personal feng shui comes from carrying the symbolic image of your horoscope allies, especially when they are going through good years.

The Boar and its allies as a group definitely need each other in 2010. You the Boar have the best rating in terms of Life Force and inner chi essence, so you are in a good position to help and assist your allies. Doing so will definitely enhance your own luck. In fact in 2010 you enjoy the favorable star number 9 which brings many good things including the chance to create a strong foundation for the future.

Helping your allies will help you overcome the 24 Mountain Robbery Star which afflicts your compass location. But the phenomenon of the alliance of allies together as a group will help you overcome cosmic afflictions such as this. It also enables you to perform better as a group than doing things as a loner. Indeed, when the alliance of allies cooperate with each other and team up, their collective positive energy gets magnified.

Hence if your business associates and you comprise this grouping of Sheep, Rabbit and Boar, the year will be easier to manage. If there are three of you in a family, or within the same department of a company, the alliance can be activated to benefit every member. In this alliance, Rabbit will be the natural leader in 2010 but you the Boar can also set an example.

Boar's confidence levels are average this year but most of you have good fortune luck according to the elements in your horoscope chart for the year. Most high vitality is the Water Boar who at 27 is ready to make big waves in 2010. For you, fortune smiles as both financial and success luck awaits - just make sure you do not bite off too much and watch your health.

## 2. Paired Soulmates

There are 6 pairs of animal signs that are described as natural soulmates. One sign is yin and the other yang. In astrology texts, they are described as creating the 6 Zodiac Houses with each one manifesting its own special niche of compatibility. The pairing creates a powerful bonding on a cosmic level, and a marriage or business union between any two people belonging to the same Zodiac House will have instant rapport with each other. There will be an inexplicable attraction! When people talk about 'falling in love at first sight' it is likely they belong to the same House, and should they marry, there is promise of great happiness for them as a family. The soulmates pairing spells happiness in a much more concentrated way than any other kind of zodiac alliance. The yin and yang of the two signs indicate the presence of intrinsic male and female essence that taps into a very special cosmic force.

This combination is also great for those who want to work together professionally – e.g. as business partners in a practice - and between siblings. The mutual strength of each pair is different, as some make better commercial partners than marriage partners. How successful you are as a pair depends on how deeply you bond and how close you allow yourselves to get with one another.

A coming together of yin Boar with its soulmate the yang Dog creates the *House of Domesticity*. It is a very lovely alliance that as a team generates wonderful family harmony, because these are two animal signs for whom home domestic bliss is more important than anything else. Family is extremely important to you, so the bond you share is very strong and powerful loyalty. A marriage between the two of you is certain to be very harmonious and happy.

In 2010 both the Dog and the Boar are not feeling particularly upbeat, but it is Boar who will be more optimistic than the two. Should you be in a commercial arrangement with one another, it benefits for Dog to trust Boar to get the job done. This is a year when Boar tends to perform much better than Dog in commercial type ventures.

## Houses of Paired Soulmates

| Animals | Yin/ Yang | Zodiac House of Creativity | Target Unleashed |
|---------|-----------|----------------------------|------------------|
| Rat | Yang | House of Creativity & Cleverness | The Rat initiates |
| Ox | Yin | | The Ox completes |
| Tiger | Yang | House of Growth & Development | The Tiger employs force |
| Rabbit | Yin | | The Rabbit uses diplomacy |
| Dragon | Yang | House of Magic & Spritituality | The Dragon creates magic |
| Snake | Yin | | The Snake creates mystery |
| Horse | Yang | House of Passion & Sexuality | The Horse embodies male energy |
| Sheep | Yin | | The Sheep is the female energy |
| Monkey | Yang | House of Career & Commerce | The Monkey creates strategy |
| Rooster | Yin | | The Rooster gets things moving |
| Dog | Yang | House of Domesticity | The Dog works to provide |
| Boar | Yin | | The Boar enjoys what is created |

## 3. Secret Friends

| Pairings of Secret Friends | | | | | |
|------|------|--------|---------|--------|-------|
| Rat | Boar | Dog | Dragon | Snake | Horse |
| Ox | Tiger | Rabbit | Rooster | Monkey | Sheep |

The third set of very special relationships in the zodiac groupings creates the bond of a secret friendship under which a very powerful astrological affinity is created. Secret friends are exceptionally compatible. This is a vigorous union of two equals and works very well as a married couple. There is love, respect and goodwill. Theirs is a bond which once forged will be hard to break; and even when they themselves want to call it quits with each other, still it will be hard for either party to fully walk away. This pair of signs will stick together through thick and thin. They are fiercely protective of each other and even when they are no longer partners, there is still some kind of lingering comradeship between them. But one will dominate and it is usually the animal sign whose *heavenly stem* element controls the other.

In the pairing of secret friends, Boar is paired with Tiger. There is a very special bond between these two animal signs and it appears like a case of opposites being very attractive to each other. They have very different personalities but find it easy to enjoy one another's company and to be intensely loyal to each other. As astrological soulmates, they naturally gravitate towards one another. A marriage between them has a chance to grow into a very happy family unit indeed. The good thing about these secret friends is that they bring out the best in each other, one inspiring the other to greater heights.

## 4. Astrological Enemies

According to principles of the Horoscope, the animal sign that directly confronts yours is your astrological enemy who can never help you. For the Boar, the enemy is the Snake. Note that the enemy does not necessarily harm you; it only means someone of this sign can never be of any real help to you. The elements of the two are conflicting; Snake is Fire and Boar is Water, so here the Snake will never be able to reach heights or go very far if married to a Boar and vice versa. The two will tend to be very competitive with one another.

## Pairings of Astrological Enemies

| Rat | Boar | Dog | Rabbit | Tiger | Ox |
|-----|------|-----|--------|-------|------|
| Horse | Snake | Dragon | Rooster | Monkey | Sheep |

There is a six year gap between the two signs and any pairing between them is unlikely to benefit either side. Whatever sincere intentions they have tends to be short lived and cannot stand the test of time. Marriage between a Boar and a Snake is generally unlikely to bring lasting happiness unless there are other indications in their respective paht chee charts. Pairings between arrows of antagonism are usually discouraged by those who investigate Zodiac compatibilities. Boars are advised to refrain from getting involved with a Snake. You will only get your heart broken!

As a business partnership, the pairing is likely to lead to problems, and in the event of a split, the separation can be acrimonious even if they start out as best friends. In 2010, any coming together of the Boar and the Snake will be unhappy, disappointing and filled with aggravations. Better not to pursue this relationship or allow it to go too far.

The Snake is the astrological foe of the Boar.

When two opposite signs have a hostile connection this way and they stay in the same house, they cannot be close; they have a completely different sets of friends. If they are siblings, they will not share confidences and will eventually drift apart. If they stay apart there will not be any direct antagonism but they are unlikely to have much in common.

## 5. Peach Blossom Links

Each of the Alliance of Allies has a special relationship with one of the four primary signs of Horse, Rat, Rooster and Rabbit in that these are the symbolic representations of love and romance for one alliance group of animal signs. In the horoscope, they are referred to as *peach blossom animals* and the presence of their images in the homes of the matching alliance of allies brings peach blossom luck which is associated with love and romance.

**The Boar belongs to the Alliance of Sheep, Rabbit and Boar, and they have the Rat as their peach blossom link. The Boar will benefit from associating with anyone born in the Rat year, and will also benefit from placing a painting or image of a Rat in the North corner of the house, or in the Boar direction of NW.**

# 6. Seasonal Trinity

There is another grouping of animal signs which creates the four seasonal trinity combinations that bring exceptional luck of seasonal abundance. To many astrology experts, this is regarded as one of the more powerful combinations of animal signs. When the combination exists within a family made up of either parent or both parents and with one or more children, they will collectively be strong enough to transform the luck indications for the family members that make up the combination, for the entire year.

This means that even when the annual indications of the year may not appear favorable, the existence of the seasonal combination of animals within any living abode is sufficient to transform the luck making it a lot better. The best times will also always be felt by the season indicated by the combination.

It is however necessary for **all three animal signs** to live together or to be in the same office working in close proximity for this powerful pattern to take effect. For greater impact, it is better feng shui if they are all using the direction associated with the relevant seasons. Thus the seasonal combination of Spring is East, while the seasonal combination of Summer is South. The Boar belongs to the seasonal combination of Winter, a combination which creates links with

## Seasonal Trinities of the Horoscope

| Animal signs | Season | Element | Direction |
|---|---|---|---|
| Dragon, Rabbit, Tiger | Spring | Wood | East |
| Snake, Horse, Sheep | Summer | Fire | South |
| Monkey, Rooster, Dog | Autumn | Metal | West |
| Ox, Rat, Boar | Winter | Water | North |

the Ox and the Rat, two signs whose affinity to each other is strong and potent. With them the Boar could feel like an outsider but their astrological ties are powerful in attracting tremendous benefits if they operate as a group.

Thus for instance, when a Rat and an Ox marry and they have a Boar child, the three of them creates the trinity of winter. This means that they are not only exceptionally close but will attract the luck of abundance during the winter season! Seasonal trinities are one of the more potent of Zodiac combinations.

# BOAR WITH RAT *(Comfortable)*
## Water Energy Works in Their Favor

The Boar enjoys a very good year materially and therefore will continue to be a reassuring presence in the Rat's life. In 2010, this is a happy couple, especially since Boar's vitality is good relative to Rat.

> The relationship between Rat and Boar arises from their being part of the *Seasonal Trinity of Winter*. This brings the condensed luck of the hibernating months to this couple. Both also belong to the Water element, which brings incredible good feng shui in 2010. **Together they signify the yin and yang of Water; which puts them in a very good place to make the most of the year's thirsty energy.**

This is a pairing of soft spoken and sensitive people; they play and work well together, generally giving in with no hesitation. The Rat and Boar are comfortable with the energy of the year, as Rat somehow stays distracted from mainstream aspirations and traditionally what it likes. As luck is on Boar's side, this is a time when going on holidays become significant.

Rat is happy to accept the generosity of Boar in 2010. For Rat in 2010, love and marriage will tend to define the year. Focus is not on career or on business, as Rat succumbs to the pleasures brought by peach blossom luck. So Boar becomes somewhat the dominant partner. In 2010, the Boar's Life Force and Spirit Essence matches that of the Rat in intensity and essence. So they are psychologically well-matched.

A pairing between the 26 year old Wood Rat with the 27 year old Water Boar benefits the Rat extremely as this young Boar is experiencing a very good year indeed, enjoying an excellent set of lucky elements. So here, Rat can share Boar's good fortune. This pair has plenty of opportunities to laugh together, enjoying each other's easy comradeship and excellent sense of humor.

For the 38 year old Water Rat and 39 year old Metal Boar, the energy levels of both are very complementary, with Boar enjoying good health and success luck and Rat having excellent financial luck.

As for the 50 year old Metal Rat and 51 year old Earth Boar, this is a partnership that will place both on an even keel. As both Rat and Boar belong to the Water element, they should jointly enjoy a year sorely lacking in Water, as it is sure to benefit them.

# BOAR WITH OX *(Nonchalant)*
## Cannot Find Common Ground

This pair of animal signs has little in common and should they meet up and come together, they find it hard to establish a comfortable feeling with each other. They cannot find the rhythm, as there seems to be very little by way of shared passions or hobbies. So they tend to leave each other quite cold.

When they meet, they will be laid back with both likely adopting an air of indifference. They are not putting on an act. This is a reflection of the lack of excitement between an Ox and a Boar. It is possible for them to be friends, but rarely will a love relationship bring out the excitement.

They also cannot generate much passion for one another. Any relationship they have is best characterized as a terrible indifference that makes this a boring relationship. In 2010, Boar appears to have a better year than the Ox, with Life Force and inner chi energy at pretty average levels when compared to the negative readings for Ox. As a result, they are unable to be in sync with each other. Ox will focus on work and end up ignoring Boar most of the time. The Boar has always been rather laid back; always unfussy and slow when it comes to work matters. So beyond the first five minutes, these two people will have precious little to chat about. Another problem is that they are not very interested in each other's opinion. So here it is not about being good or bad for each other; there is just no spark ignited between them. Nothing that one does will stimulate the other, so they find each other rather dull. Those who just met will probably split after a couple of outings.

Humor is missing, so a challenging Tiger Year is sure to be tough for this couple. They will be too serious, unable to use laughter to get them through the year. Both of you deserve better than to be stuck with someone so unsuitable for you!

The advice is to focus on how to make the most of the year on your own. It should not be necessary to depend on a partner and in any case, this is a year when both the Boar and Ox work better as loners. Setting time aside for contemplation and serious strategic thinking is more worthwhile. For those already married to each other, try to find a comfort zone and then get on with your life.

The year 2010 is not a great year for Boar as energy levels are negative. You will be lethargic about many of your relationships and you will need something special to galvanize you. It is unlikely that the year will oblige.

# BOAR WITH TIGER *(Excellent)*
## Secret Friends with Excellent Ho Tu

With the Boar, the Tiger has a great and extremely satisfying relationship, and in 2010, they will find wonderful and exhilarating companionship with one another. It will be a year when they discover just how stimulating they each can be as they inspire one another to overcome the negativities of the year and go forward bravely and surely. What is needed is confidence and reassurance, and since they can rely on each other to bounce ideas off of, the year can very likely turn out to be exciting for them indeed.

These two are not just the secret friends of the zodiac but in 2010, they also enjoy the added benefits of **having their feng shui numbers create the all powerful and auspicious Ho Tu combination.** In the feng shui chart, Tiger is 2 and Boar is 9 and 2/9 combines to bring good news for the pair.

Th 2/9 Ho Tu brings them amazing and unexpected good fortune, and the Ho Tu is also powerful enough to override all other negative afflictions. What this means is that as a couple, the Tiger and Boar can quite effectively overcome whatever negativities may be brought to them as a result of feng shui afflictions and element mismatches.

Even without the Ho Tu they are already one of the more successful pairings of the zodiac. The Tiger and Boar enjoy very similar attitudes. They can see the good side of any development or event, and they are good at making the best of whatever comes their way. They are positive people who know how to extract good energy from challenging times. The year is going to be a challenging one for many people, but together, they can ride out any challenges they may encounter.

Indeed Boar's horoscope chart does not show very good indications. Neither is Tiger's chart looking particularly good; nevertheless, they will not suffer very negative swings in fortune in 2010.

The good thing about the Tiger and Boar union is how secure they are with each other. They do not have hidden agendas, nor do they harbor childish suspicions that lead to tensions and recriminations. Theirs is a very straightforward relationship where a lifetime commitment to one another is an easy thing.

Those of you in your twenties should get as much as you can out of the Tiger Year. There is money to be made and fortunes to be built. 2010 is as good a year as any to get started; and if you are lucky enough to be in a relationship with a Boar, make the most of it.

# BOAR WITH RABBIT *(Exceptional)*
## Boar Brings Good Fortune

This is a very happy twosome whose respect and love for one another is inspiring and infectious. Their attitude to life is happily relaxed and easy going, so for them, outside influences do not affect their commitment towards each other.

In 2010, Boar brings exceptional good fortune to Rabbit as its Water element feeds a thirsty Wood Rabbit! Apart from this significant matter, their energies are also nicely balanced and there will be no major developments to cause them problems with each other. Negativities are kept to a minimum. As a result the year flows smooth and steady for them and although they may not be experiencing an exceptionally special time in 2010, it is also not going to be a bad year either.

The Rabbit is not at its best in 2010, but then neither will be the Boar. Both are in sync when it comes to being wary of the year of the Tiger. This will make them careful and encourage them not to take too many risks but it does not cause them to be immobile or inactive. Besides, both have the much needed water element brought by the Boar! And this will make quite a crucial difference. This is also what binds them so close to one another.

As a team they work and survive well together, so if anything, the Year of the Tiger will bring this couple closer than ever to each other. This is a good time for their trust in one another to manifest a solidarity that makes them tougher and more effective.

> Rabbit and Boar make up two thirds of the alliance of allies known as the Diplomats of the Zodiac. For them, going through a ferocious year will be the same as going through any other year. As long as they are together, they take the good with the bad with equanimity.

In 2010 they lean equally on each other with neither having an edge over the other. The 23 year old Fire Rabbit will be especially drawn to the 27 year old Water Boar should they be meeting for the first time. These two will find the year pans out well for them as both have a good share of financial as well as success luck.

The Rabbit and Boar in their thirties do not enjoy as good a time as their counterparts in their twenties, but because of their natural closeness, they should weather the year equally well. Meanwhile, Boars attached to 47 year old Water Rabbit will share this Rabbit's great good fortune during the year.

# BOAR WITH DRAGON *(Grudgingly)*
## Dragon Finds An Unlikely Friend

In 2010, Dragon finds an unlikely and unexpected friend in the Boar. When thrown together, they discover an interest in each other that is fueled by charming words spoken by Dragon in praise of Boar.

This will be especially beneficial when the overture is coming from the 22 year old Earth Dragon who casts romantic eyes and flirtatious attentions on the 27 year old Water Boar. It is likely that any and all overtures made by Dragon are sure to meet with success. In fact, this young couple benefit each other so much they will find themselves sliding easily, or maybe grudgingly, into a relationship.

In 2010, the Water Boar is very attractive indeed, whether it be a gentleman or lady, and this is due mainly to a better than average horoscope chart. Fiancé luck is at its maximum and there will also be welcome success vibes. The year looks exciting and glorious. No wonder it catches the eye of the Dragon who is constantly on the lookout for fresh conquests.

Unlike last year, Boar has become stronger in 2010, and its attitude this year tends to be more upbeat. Dragon will respond in a like manner, so as a couple, the year encourages them along. In 2010, Boar's Life

Force and Spirit Essence are at very average levels, neither negative nor positive.

A pairing between the 22 year old Earth Dragon with the 26 year old Water Boar fares well this year, better than last year, but Boar might get bored and move on. For the 34 year old Fire Dragon and 39 year old Metal Boar, if they are married, the year brings wonderful complimentarity of forces which is beneficial for them both.

Better yet of one is born in either person's sign at the Hour of Birth, so that is worth checking out, because this combination looks promising, transforming a normally difficult combination into a happy and beneficial one.

The partnership bodes well for both, with Dragon enjoying Finance Luck and Boar enjoying Success Luck. This enables them to move in rhythm with each other and helps them to sail easily and happily through the year.

The 46 year old Wood Dragon and 51 year old Earth Boar also enjoy good complimentarity of luck and are likely to do well as a couple, both as business partners as well as in a romantic relationship.

# BOAR WITH SNAKE *(Unpleasant)*
## Enmity Surfaces Strongly

With Snake riding so high in 2010, Boar is sure to stay far away if it knows what's good for it. Between these two signs there really is no love lost. Indeed, Snake has the greatest clash of wills with Boar who is its natural enemy in the astrological charts.

In 2010 Snake could be tempted to turn nasty as Boar always brings out the worst in this sign.

In 2010, Snake is strong and Boar is less so. The Boar is Water while Snake is Fire, but despite the Boar signifying Water, the element that brings wealth and success to the Snake, Snake will simply extract whatever goodness is in Boar, then leave it high and dry.

The Snake in its moment of triumph will turn its back on the Boar. Such is the extent of the enmity between them. The Boar always says the wrong things to the Snake.

Should these two people ever come together in a marriage, it will be a terrible mismatch, and in 2010, it could become miserable for the Boar. This is a year when everything is going right for Snake and many things are going wrong for Boar.

One is riding high full of confidence and vitality while the other endures yin chi brought by the 24 mountains. In its element horoscope chart, the Boar has barely average Life Force luck this year, and its inner chi essence is also average. Thus the Boar is definitely no match for the strong and powerful Snake this year.

The 21 year old Earth Snake might well respond positively to the overtures of the 27 year old Water Boar and this is because this Boar will have the self assurance that comes with good prosperity energy.

If this couple does commit and get into a relationship, it is a match that is unlikely to last and over the longer term, and it will be the Snake who will bring heartache to the Boar. In 2010 however, Boar is strong enough to handle the high maintenance Snake, but it is wise to be wary!

As for those of you in your thirties, the 33 year old Fire Snake is definitely much too savvy and strong for the 39 year old Metal Boar. There is little future for these two signs and it is probably advisable for both sides to just walk away. Otherwise you are just delaying the inevitable and could end up badly hurt in the process.

# BOAR WITH HORSE *(Harmonious)*
## Solid & Dependable Pair

The Horse and Boar personify the essence of their elements - Fire and Water - being direct opposites in both appearance and personality, with one being fast and fiery – a hot head; and the other slow and steady - a cool head. But they can live and work together amicably and with great success and happiness. Over time they develop a special kind of respect and even a tolerance for one another's foibles. This arises as much from the good natured sensitivity of the Boar, who generally is an easy going person, as from the steadfast loyalty of the Horse.

Despite any number of temper tantrums, the Horse and Boar eventually kiss and make up. These two do not hold grudges. So even though the Horse can be bad tempered and impatient (as they are in 2010) there are unlikely to be any severe problems arising between them.

Horse is an action-oriented, impulsive creature while Boar tends to be a little more circumspect and careful, usually thinking things through before acting. Sometimes Boar may be regarded as being too slow and indecisive by Horse, but they agree to meet halfway and common sense often prevails; so the relationship works well most of the time. There are few contentious issues. They are comfortable with each other and are generally not too demanding. Their interactions are civil and arguments are rarely allowed to descend into a shouting match. So this is a nicely balanced relationship where giving and taking is fairly well shared between the two.

In 2010, Boar's horoscope chart is average with both high and low moments. The feng shui chart brings the lucky star 9 which can magnify good as well as bad things. Generally, Boar should be extra careful in 2010 so it does not get robbed or fall victim to petty thieves. Confidence levels are not too low but Boar suffers from a pervasive air of yin chi which seems to have carried over from last year. Horse must do more to cheer up the despondent Boar.

The 20 year old Metal Horse can happily hook up with the 27 year old Water Boar and it will turn out a good match. Here Boar enjoys a lucky year, and its horoscope elements bring some good fortune to the Horse. This pair can be happy together. But for those in their thirties - the 39 year old Metal Boar married to or in partnership with the 32 year old Earth Horse - are better off depending on the luck and judgement of the Horse. It is the same for the other relationships of Horse and Boar.

# BOAR WITH SHEEP *(Favorable)*
## Romance & Comfort with Your Ally

The Sheep goes through a troubled year but finds solace and comfort with its astrological ally, the Boar. Well suited and compatible, this couple enjoys a natural affinity that transcends the setbacks of daily life. In 2010, both experience the good and bad of the Tiger Year with Sheep feeling the brunt of it. But with the help of Boar, Sheep survives 2010 with a sense of humor. Sheep feels fortified and practical as ever, because there is love enough to help Sheep make it through the nights.

What this pair enjoys is a relaxed and easy relationship, the kind of comfort level which make them true soulmates. They experience joy in each other's company and can also forge a work relationship that is both supportive and helpful. **There is a partnership that works with little effort and should they be married to one another, it is a happy union.** They will make it easily through the Tiger Year.

This is because the Sheep and Boar make up two thirds of the group of allies that are described as the Diplomats of the Zodiac. They share a love of the gentle lifestyle which mirrors their desire for a life of quiet elegance. They communicate on similar wavelengths and are sensitive of each other's needs and feelings.

Should the young 19 year old Metal Sheep get together with the 27 year old Water Boar, the attraction will be instant, with Boar taking the lead, guiding and caring for Sheep all the way. This will be a beautiful match, with Sheep bringing out all the protective instincts of Boar. They will be inseparable in 2010.

The 31 year old Earth Sheep meanwhile enjoys a strong set of elements which brings great health, moderate financial and good success luck. This Sheep does better with the 27 year old Water Boar but has just as good a rapport with the 39 year old Metal Boar.

For the older Sheep and Boar people, the year brings a variety of luck patterns that make it easy for them to complement each other. Generally however, Boar has a stronger and more auspicious year than Sheep. Nevertheless, there is excellent synergy between them and through the year, just by being together, they will find many of the disappointments a lot easier to cope with. They are thus excellent for one another.

# BOAR WITH MONKEY *(Beneficial)*
## Must Try to Stay True

This is a complementary relationship between two different personalities. The Monkey and Boar do great things for one another's ego, but in terms of what turns them on, their tastes and preferences cannot be more different. Their attitudes towards life are different but they do complement one another and this is the basis of their attraction for each other. Despite the Monkey and Boar liking different things they naturally gravitate to each other should they meet.

The Monkey is drawn to Boar's philosophy of life which is easy going. It is an attitude of relaxed acceptance of all of life's indulgences which the Monkey secretly identifies with. Meanwhile, the Monkey is a sign that is universally admired and Boar is no exception. Should Monkey do the pursuing, Boar is likely to offer a positive response. And despite Boar feeling just a little bit in awe of Monkey, nevertheless Boar will be keen to develop a relationship with Monkey.

This couple is inspired by different people and interests, and should they come together as a couple, it will be a case of opposites attracting. In 2010, the energy levels of Boar and Monkey are different, with

Monkey alert and full of vitality while Boar's is at a more sedate level. Monkey is quite hyper despite the year being rather difficult and filled with a variety of afflictions.

Boar on the other hand has a very average year in terms of its pattern of luck based on elements. The feng shui chart likewise brings a year of mixed signals for Boar indicating that while there are good moments, there is also a Small Robbery Star to contend with brought by the 24 Mountains. But Boar is going through the Tiger Year and the Tiger is the secret friend of the Boar, hence there is hidden cosmic support. Boar will benefit Monkey this year.

Those who are married are likely to have to endure some tensions as Monkey will have a tendency to flirt and create noise levels outside the marriage. Boar might not be in a forgiving mood and there could be trouble. Monkey is a flirtatious sign and not adverse to the idea of some "harmless fun", but this is not how Boar would view it.

The 27 Water Boar is definitely not in the mood to accept any kind of infidelity from its Monkey partner… so if it is the 30 year old Metal Monkey involved, the advice is for Monkey to not mess with its Boar spouse or partner.

# BOAR WITH ROOSTER *(Helpful)*
## Very Strongly Benefiting the Boar

In 2010, the Rooster is helping the Boar all the way. In a year when both its luck and its chi energy are at an all time high, Rooster finds itself being especially generous and beneficial to the Boar. These are two exceptionally different people with almost nothing in common, yet the Rooster feels unaccountably protective.

Much of the compatibility here arises from the Boar's non-confrontational approach to winning the Rooster. Sedate and clam, it is a perfect foil for the Rooster's noisy approach to everything. In the Tiger Year, Rooster has many excellent indications in the chart - from Big Auspicious stars brought by the 24 Mountains to a horoscope pattern of elements that is the envy of many other signs. The Rooster is thus strong and tough and on a roll.

In the Boar, Rooster finds satisfaction because the Boar makes Rooster feel needed and useful. Boar brings out the protective instinct in Rooster and does it in a diplomatic way. Boar is motivated by a genuine admiration for Rooster. As such, the interaction between these two signs is pleasant and delightful. It appeals to the softer side of Rooster, so one can say that Boar charms the Rooster.

Usually when a Boar succeeds in snaring a Rooster, it will hold on tight and never let go. The Boar is clever, and astute enough to see the benefits of pairing with the Rooster. In 2010 this belief pays dividends because Rooster will enhance the luck of Boar very substantially indeed.

> In 2010, the energy levels of the Rooster and the Boar favor the Rooster. In this marriage between Rooster and Boar, it is the Rooster who will be the strength that holds them together.

The 17 year old Water Rooster is on a roll this year but may be too young to want to commit to a steady relationship.

The 29 year old Wood Rooster will benefit the 27year old Water Boar. This is the same story all the way for the other couples and this is mainly due to the productive relationship their stem elements have with each other.

This is a very beneficial pairing for them in 2010, especially for the Boar, as Rooster's luck holds the promise of something big and exciting on the horizon.

# BOAR WITH DOG *(Going With the Flow)*
## Making the Most of the Tiger Year

The Dog and Boar each has a very special link with the Tiger whose year it is! The Dog is the Tiger's ally while the Boar is the Tiger's secret friend. Hence the year smiles on these two signs despite them being rather lacking in the energy department.

From the feng shui chart however, we do see that these two signs share the auspicious number of 9 which brings completion luck as well as recognition and promotion. 9 is an auspicious number as it suggests that whatever gets built this year has a good chance of doing well. So as a pair, they will find the year beneficial for them as a couple.

Dog gets along with Boar not in any insanely passionate way, but **they have an easy relationship which contains trust and support in good measure**. They rarely quarrel or have misunderstandings although Dog's energy in 2010 is at an all-time low, and that of Boar is not very high. Happily for them, they will find ways to compensate for whatever energy shortfall afflicts them.

Dog is attracted to the untroubled and unruffled way Boar goes about the business of living. There is a great deal of sincerity on both sides with neither judging the other and both agreeing to allow the other to have their own space.

In 2010 the pair in their twenties - the 28 year old Water Dog and the 27 year old Water Boar - have plenty to look forward to. Financially and professionally, they enjoy a great year marked by happiness occasions. Working life holds many things to excite them so it is beneficial for them to be workaholic. It is good not to miss the main chance.

The couple in their thirties i.e. the 40 year old Metal Dog and 39 year old Metal Boar find the Boar having a better year, but they enjoy the year nevertheless.

The Dog and Boar in their fifties have rather lopsided energies. They are sure to take a more mature and responsible attitude to looking after their health and Boar enjoys excellent health luck. Those in their sixties have the funds to indulge and protect themselves.

# BOAR WITH BOAR *(Kind)*
## Being A Lot More Pleasant

Happily those born to the sign of the Boar have a vested interest in making the most of the Tiger Year, the year ruled by their secret friend. So it is definitely beneficial to subdue any feelings of envy, no matter how well camouflaged these may be. Boars tend to be very sensitive about each other's failings, but it is also not difficult for them to be kind to their own signs, there being a natural affinity between them.

Somehow the Boar feels the eccentricities of others more acutely than they care to admit and they sometimes take delight in pointing out the faults of those close to them. The more they get a reaction, the more they tend to go on and on about and continue harping on the same things.

The Boar is also a sign that will not let anyone have the last word and so if they live together, two Boars are sure to reflect off each other's self centered attitudes. In 2010, it is advisable to actively watch against being excessively critical of each other. It is much better to be pleasant and kind.

The sad thing is that despite making a resolution not to go headlong at one another, they do have to work hard to ensure that whatever disagreements they have do not quickly degenerate into confrontational situations.

In 2010 the Boar enjoys the luck of completion so it is a year when some seriously excellent career developments could take place. But energy levels are only average, so it is advisable not to waste your chi on negative pursuits.

Those of you who are married to each other will discover that 2010 continues to be a year when mutual support is not just advisable; it is **crucial** to your good fortune this year.

Those in their fifties, sixties and seventies will find that while there is success luck benefiting your work situation, on the money side there could be some problems. Economically, the horoscope scenario allows them to enjoy the year but Boars being Boars, no matter what happens, they are not the worrying type. So no matter what the challenges of the year may be, Boars are generally pretty laid back.

Teenager and Boars in their twenties are going through a good time and are certain to find social life very enjoyable. The 27 Water Boar have excellent finance and success luck and will either grow closer or become intensely competitive with each other.

# Part 3
# Boar's Monthly Horoscope 2010

The Boar person this year enjoys the number 9 star which signifies future prosperity. This makes 2010 a good year for laying the groundwork for the future. The business outlook for Boar born people is thus quite good.

However, Boar gets hit by the **Robbery Star** from the 24 Mountains, hence could suffer from losses and being cheated in 2010. It is thus wise not to place too much trust in anyone and to display the **Water Globe** cure in your home location of NW.

Career luck for the Boar is steady; this is a good year to consolidate job responsibilities. There are also months when you enjoy the **sum-of-ten** which brings you auspicious money luck.

# 1ST MONTH
## February 4th - March 5th 2010

### YOU HAVE LOW LEVEL OF TOLERANCE THIS MONTH

This is a busy month for the Boar with plenty to get done. Watch you don't get overly flustered or stress could overcome you. You are more quick tempered than usual, and may find it difficult to get along with others. Working in a team may prove difficult. Hostilities with workmates and colleagues could arise making things difficult at the office. It is important to try and subdue your bad temper. Go with the flow. Take a holiday to get away if you have to. Don't engage yourself in any big fights as your luck is down and victory is uncertain. Wait till the quarrelsome energies of this month cease before trying to reconcile any differences. There is also danger of litigation. If you are sued, the advice is to settle out of court.

### WORK & CAREER – *Could Get Noisy*

Things at the office could get noisy this month. Blow ups with colleagues could occur due to your argumentative nature this month. While you may find it difficult to get along with others, they probably think the same thing about you. Learn to relax. This month it is wiser to work on your own and to avoid too much group work. Schedule important meetings for another time if you can. This month, the less said the better, because what comes out of your mouth could be your downfall. Lie low and let the hostile energies of the month pass.

## BUSINESS – *Fierce Competition*

There is indication of much fiercer competition than you are used to on the horizon. Resist fraternizing with the enemy lest you let on too much or lose your cool in conversation. If you are involved in much contact with your business associates, carry a Wor Peng amulet to help keep your energies calm and to protect you against saying the wrong things. Avoid signing agreements or entering into partnerships or joint ventures this month. Document everything in black and white to ensure you are legally protected, but leave signing on the dotted line till after the end of this month. Display an Eight Legged

Display the Eight Legged Lion in the NW of your office for smoother relationships in the workplace.

Lion in the NW of your office to control the hostile energies of the month.

## LOVE & RELATIONSHIPS – *Romance Fizzles Out*

Romance fizzles out due mostly to your irksome mood. You may think you are being reasonable but your partner may be done putting up with your mood swings and could need some space. The problem with you right now is that you don't seem to know what you want. You can't seem to get along with other people, but yet you want them around. You need someone to listen, but you're unwilling to listen back. Work a bit harder at being a good companion if you want good companionship back. And if you're looking for romance, you're going to have to do a lot to earn it this month!

## SCHOOL & EDUCATION – *Keep Your Cool*

Things may be a little tough for the young Boar because of the quarrelsome energies that surround you. Try not to get too worked up over issues. It is not worth it. If you disagree with your parents or teachers on what you have planned for yourself, take a long hard look at why you want to do things your way. When you analyze it that way, your point of view may not seem so good after all.

# 2ND MONTH
## March 6th - April 4th 2010

### HEALTH LUCK VERY LOW; YOUNG CHILDREN BE CAREFUL

Watch out for the illness star this month. The coming four weeks is particular dangerous for the young Boar, so children should be more careful. Wear a **Wu Lou amulet** to protect yourself against falling sick. Avoid taking unnecessary risks and make it a point to watch your health. Eat well and get enough rest. You may find yourself getting distracted at work due to fatigue. Watch you keep a good balance in your life and don't push yourself too hard when your immunity and defenses are down. Success does not come easy this month. For the Boar in business, the yin energies of the month bring obstacles and problems. Avoid doing too much in a month when your luck levels are at such a low ebb. Instead, wait till things improve next month, when the outlook is much much better.

## WORK & CAREER – *Easily Distracted*
You find yourself easily distracted this month. Getting enough sleep could also prove a problem, and

this makes you less productive at work the next day. Try to rearrange your lifestyle to fit in enough rest as you are physically weaker this period. You have good opportunities ahead of you this month, but a lack of ability to focus could cost you these breaks.

Watch out for careless mistakes. If you're involved in tedious work, it will be easy to slip up. You may forget things causing you to be unreliable. Watch you don't make too many blunders too often or your ratings with the boss could slide. This is not a good time to volunteer to take on more tasks at work. Don't make life even more difficult for yourself. Leave your impressing tactics to another time. You're not a hero right now, do don't try to be.

## BUSINESS – *Cloudy Judgment*
Business luck for the Boar person reflects the yin energies affecting your chart this month. Try not to schedule too many important meetings now as fatigue may cloud your judgment. Avoid making significant changes to the way you run things. If you work in an industry where risk of injury is high, take it slow. Take more steps to minimize risk because risk of injury is higher this month. Success does not come easily. Be patient, as prospects look much improved next month.

## LOVE & RELATIONSHIPS – *Ditch the Superficial*

Things look better for the Boar when it comes to love. This month favor Boars in steady relationships. If you're involved with someone, chances are you will really see eye to eye this month, and you are able to take your relationship to a new level. Get to know each other more intimately. An amalgamation of minds is what will make your union truly special. If the two of you don't have too much in common besides physical attraction, you may start to lose interest.

For the single Boar, ditch the superficial and go for what's real. Your tastes may mature this month, causing you to fall for a platonic friend! Don't rule out relationships of this kind as they could turn out to be just what you've been looking for.

## HEALTH & WELLNESS– *Illness Energies*

Carry a **health amulet** or Wu Lou this month to protect against falling sick. Illness caused by the number 2 star in your chart can get serious, so take this advice seriously. If you feel something is not right, it is better to go for a check up just to be on the safe side. Be more careful when taking part in dangerous sports. Avoid taking risks. Eat well and look after yourself.

# 3RD MONTH
## April 5th - May 5th 2010

### EXCELLENT GROWTH OPPORTUNITIES

A truly auspicious month awaits the Boar person! The **sum-of-ten** in your chart brings excellent growth opportunities. Money luck is promising and career luck is good. There are opportunities for self development and improvement. This is also a lucky time for the young Boar in school. Many things go right for you this month, so don't hold back. Be confident. The surer you are of yourself, the more you can get out of this month. There is also transformation luck in your chart, so you can expect some changes to occur in your life. Go with the flow and you'll be pleasantly surprised where you end up.

### WORK & CAREER – *All Systems Go*

Relationships at the office are excellent this month. It's all systems go at work and the more you are in charge of, the happier you are! You feel a lot healthier and fitter this month, and your mind is more focused. You're efficient and on the ball, making you a joy to work with. Taking charge comes naturally to you and those of you in managerial roles will really get to shine this month. There is promotion luck which you can enhance with a **Monkey on a Horse** figurine, or if you are vying for a top job, a **Monkey on an Elephant**. Display these symbols on your work desk. This is a month when putting in additional effort is worthwhile. Aim to impress by performing your job well, not by talking yourself up.

## BUSINESS – *Deal Making*

Many new opportunities are suggesting themselves to you. If you've wrapped up some longstanding projects recently, you are going to want to have something substantial to sink your teeth into now. That's why you are shopping around for good ideas. You're in innovator mode, and are happy to leave routine, operational matters in the hands of your managers. You on the other hand are happiest deal making and sniffing out new opportunities.

Your make a strong leader this month, so use this as a chance to motivate and galvanize your staff. If you are heading a large company, dedicate time to getting to know all your employees, not just the ones working directly under you. This is also a good time to talk business with potential business partners. You're very convincing when you speak and cutting a good deal will be easy for you, especially with the luck of the sum-of-ten on your side.

## LOVE & RELATIONSHIPS – *A Time for Change*

This is a month when love can truly blossom if you let it. Seize the initiative to forge ahead onto newer pastures if you've recently ended something. A change this month is just what you need, so start changing the way you think, dress and speak, if you have to. As long as you keep enjoying yourself, you are doing things right.

For the married Boar, your relationship with your spouse may go through some transformation, but both of you will come out better from it. If you've had unspoken issues you've been wanting to talk to your spouse about, this is a good time to spill the beans and let your feelings out.

## SCHOOL & EDUCATION – *A Blast!*

You're going to have an absolute blast this month! There are lots of new activities to get involved with and you excel in almost anything you put your mind to. Extracurricular activities suit you well this month, so get involved in the clubs and societies that your school has to offer. Because the energies in your chart spell change for the better, don't be surprised if you have a change of heart for one of your pet-hate subjects. Something you used to find difficult could suddenly become fun, and easy!

# 4TH MONTH
## May 6th - June 5th 2010

### SUCCESS LUCK GETS MAGNIFIED!

This is a fast paced month for the Boar. Goals get achieved and dreams can come true. Make sure you have time to focus on what you want. If you let yourself roll along with the humdrum of daily life, you could miss a good chance to go after what you really want. Some of you may be perfectly happy with the way you are, but those of you who are hungry for success should not let the auspicious energies of the month go to waste. You're feeling fighting fit and have the stamina for hard work. Pursue what you're going for with passion and success will come quite easily.

### WORK & CAREER – *Don't Make Enemies*

There may be someone at work that has the knack of getting your goat up. You'll get your chance to put your antagonist in his or her place. But while getting your own back may be hard to resist, tone down your tongue if you're thinking more long-term than short-term in your current job. You may win this round, but making enemies won't help your cause if your luck takes a dive and things get rough down the line. Don't burn any bridges for a few moments satisfaction. The thought of retribution may be sweet but the reality usually isn't.

## BUSINESS – *Exciting Times*

These are exciting times for the Boar in business. This is a high publicity month where those of you who know how to benefit from media will go far. Keep up your enthusiasm. If asked for interviews, accept. Social and business networking will also help you this month. Of all the new people you'll be meeting, there are at least one or two you'll keep in touch with outside the cocktail parties and soirees. They may even become future business partners.

Because publicity luck is good, this is the right time to launch an advertising or publicity campaign. Plan your strategies carefully and you can gain plenty of ground. Because your luck is on an upward trend, you can afford to invest and expand. However, because things are going well, you may be tempted to act without thinking things properly through. Don't be overly impulsive when making decisions, but at the same time don't be too conservative either.

## LOVE & ROMANCE – *Passion Rules!*

Passion rules and there's much to make your heart race! Expect numerous opportunities to forget everything else and follow your heart. You can afford to do that if you're young without a care in the world, but for if you have responsibilities in life, make a conscious effort not to neglect them. This month can be deceptive because you're riding a chart filled with lucky stars. Be as wild and outrageous as you want but don't do anything that you could regret later on.

## SCHOOL & EDUCATION – *Turbo-Charged*

The Boar in school benefits from the turbo-charged energies of the month. You do well both academically as well as in sports and any other extracurricular activities. This month could see you get a meaningful award if you've been working towards it. This is a lucky month to think about scholarships and other accolades you can win.

## HOME & FAMILY – *Find a Balance*

The social circuit beckons and you land yourself more party invitations than you can handle. This is a good time to network, but spare some time for the family. The energies this month are heady but don't let your popularity get to your head. Focus on balance. Divide your time up between work, friends and family, but don't let family take a back seat. If you're married, think about rekindling emotional bonds with your spouse. Meaningful conversations inside the family will bring positive things into your life.

# 5TH MONTH
## June 6th - July 6th 2010

### INCOME INCREASES & FOUNDATION FOR FUTURE GETS LAID

Everything you do goes right this month. This is a great time if you're looking to start new ventures, put plans into motion, or try something you've always wanted to. Both current and future prosperity gets enhanced this month. You'll be having a good time because not only do you have good income luck, you also know exactly what you want to spend that extra cash on! Things fall into place for you without you having to do much at all. When good things happen, don't question too much. Just enjoy!

### WORK & CAREER — *More Responsibilities*

You may be given more responsibilities at work. This is a first step to the promotion you may be working towards. Your working relationship with your boss reaches a new level. You connect at a higher level and he or she treats you more like a confidante. Money luck is excellent. This could be a time when your job is not your only source of income. Watch however that if you're making money on the side that it does not clash with your work commitments or terms of employment. You don't want to ruin your good luck this month with mess-ups of this kind.

## BUSINESS – *Think Forward*

Financial luck is strong this month, and there will be less to stress you out. Risks taken in the past prove themselves good ones. If you run a well-established business where routine has overtaken innovation and new ideas, this is a good time to reintroduce some forward-thinking strategies. Continue to benefit from the systems that are already in place, but be brave. By introducing some good new ideas, you could augment sales and income by a sizeable amount. Partnerships struck up now will go well. There is a large vein of wealth waiting to be tapped, and this month you have the luck to tap it!

## LOVE & RELATIONSHIPS – *Be Honest*

This promises to be a great month for love and all matters concerning the heart. If you have spotted the target of your affections, don't hold back your feelings! This is a good month to be honest and open about how you feel. If you've been dating, you may be thinking of taking things a step further. The energies of the month favor weddings, proposals and firming up relationships. Single Boars on the look out could meet someone they can really connect with.

## SCHOOL & EDUCATION – *Gaining Confidence*

Things continue going well for the Boar in school. Your confidence is up and you find learning easy and also a joy. This is a good time to learn to work independently. You may be expected to take on a large project on your own. This may be coursework that counts toward your end of year report or some other important assignment. You will relish the task once you get into it.

There is much competitive spirit in you this month. Use that competitive energy in your schoolwork but do not let the pressure to do well get to you. You are truly on a roll this month and every bit of hard work you put in will be worth it once the results come back.

## HOME & FAMILY – *Building Ties*

Family may feature more prominently in your life. Make it a point to get to know some of your more distant relatives. This is a good time to strengthen your ties with extended family. If you make an effort, you will surprise yourself at how much you have in common. A distant family member could wind up doing you a favor this month. Don't refuse help when it is offered to you.

# 6TH MONTH
## July 7th - Aug 7th 2010

**DO NOT CHANGE JOBS
OR EMPLOY NEW PEOPLE**

The excess Metal in your chart causes this to be a volatile month. Human interpersonal and behavioral problems cause some worry. This is not a good time to employ new people, nor a time to place too much trust in anyone. The violent star 7 brings hostile energy that can manifest in the form of burglary, violence or loss. Avoid taking risks. Try not to overexert yourself or expose yourself to viruses. Refrain from visiting hospitals, graveyards or attend funerals this month. The yin energy could prove too strong for you. All Boar born should wear some sort of **mantra protection** this month.

## WORK & CAREER – *Office Politics*

Things may become unstable and more difficult at work. There may be office politics to deal with. Interaction between yourself and your co-workers may become tense. Try not to be tempted to retaliate. Don't let yourself get sucked into the politics of the workplace. This month it is better to concentrate on the job at hand than to play mind games. However, you do need people on your side and need to know what's going on. Be alert to the undercurrents of the workplace and stay savvy. Note that even if things get tough, this is a bad month to think about changing jobs. Stick it out as things improve greatly next month.

## BUSINESS – *Avoid Socializing for Business*

Business luck takes a dip. You're having a spate of bad luck that attracts the wrong kind of people into your life. Don't be surprised if you are approached by people wanting to do business with you, strike a deal, or offer you something too good to be true. But any kind of offer made to you at this time should be viewed with suspicion. In fact, the safer and more bona fide the person approaching you, the more wary you should be! This is a month when your best bet is to lie low and avoid socializing for business.

Wear some mantra protection to protect against loss and harm. This Om Mani Prayer Wheel pendant opens up to contain 1.38 million consecrated mantras in microfilm, thus is extremely sacred and powerful as a protective amulet.

By all means attend parties and do's, but keep conversations entertaining and simple. Don't try to talk business at a social function. Avoid investing, taking risks and spending too much money this month. Keep things at work ticking over as usual, but don't try to introduce anything new to the business. Leave that for next month.

## LOVE & ROMANCE – *Lackluster*

Luck in love is a little lackluster this month. This is no time to make the big moves or declare your undying love to an unsuspecting soul. You could find yourself being let down, and with your disposition this month, that could be hard to take. Don't set yourself up for disappointment. Leave your quest for true love till another time.

If you're already in a steady relationship, you may find this a frustrating month. Squabbles happen for no particular reason and you're just not in your usual jovial mood. Strengthen your luck in love by carrying the double happiness symbol this month. To make it more powerful, get your partner to carry it as well. This will allow the both of you to weather the emotional storms ahead. There is much more happiness next month, so don't despair.

# 7TH MONTH
## Aug 8th - Sept 7th 2010

### SOMEONE POWERFUL COMES TO YOUR AID

The coming month sees plenty of new opportunities opening up for you. Look out for powerful new people entering your life. You could catch the eye of a powerful mentor figure who is in a position to help you. Business and career luck is promising. Good fortune comes repeatedly and once you get going, you find yourself really on a roll!

Since you have excellent mentor luck this month, if there is someone in your life who can fill that position for you, count yourself lucky and make the most of it. The good thing this month is that others want to help you. When your luck is riding high, make the most of it by being courageous. You may have to make some sacrifices with your lifestyle and your time, but it will be more than worthwhile.

### WORK & CAREER – *Support from the Boss*

Things at the work place are very pleasant for you this month because you have solid backing from your boss. You do everything right and you're the next protégé that seems to be being groomed for better things in the company. Keep up your enthusiasm and you'll find yourself really going places.

When you're treated special, jealousy is bound to arise in some form or other. Handle envious colleagues by being super nice, but don't succumb to any snide remarks on their part. Don't let them shake your confidence. You are good, so don't forget that. Boost the luck of allies and supporters by carrying your **horoscope friends and allies** with you as a personal amulet.

## BUSINESS – *Sealing Deals*

Wealth luck is looking up! Sealing big deals and winning major contracts are all possible right now, so be ambitious when pitching for jobs. Don't think too small when it comes to business. You're riding a wave of success and if you're going to ride it well, you have to throw out your conservative streak and start being brave. This is a good time to embark on new ventures, invest, expand and be bold and creative in the way you do things.

You may meet somebody influential in the course of your networking with the potential to lift your business to the next level. Don't be half-hearted about pursuing leads. If you persevere, you have a good chance of getting whatever it is you envisage for your company. Even if you don't get everything, you'll get something.

## LOVE & RELATIONSHIPS – *Flirty*

Your good mood makes it easy for others to love you! Your energetic spark is extremely contagious and you'll find the people around you perking up to match your vivacious mood this month. You enjoy being around people right now. If you're single, you're probably happiest flirting with a good number of potential suitors and developing a relationship with a special someone. Have fun this month and leave settling down for another time. You're not ready to belong to anybody right now.

## EDUCATION – *Benefit from Advice*

You benefit from advice from those older and more experienced than you. You may have to make decisions that affect the future of your academic career. Take this seriously. Talk through your options with your parents and teachers before deciding. They are in a good position to advise you. Don't try to do everything yourself or you could end up making a bad decision.

# 8TH MONTH
## Sept 8th - Oct 7th 2010

### MINOR ARGUMENTS
### ESCALATE INTO BIG FIGHTS

The month ahead looks tough as there is misfortune indicated in your chart. Bad luck can arise in all kinds of ways, so watch your step and lie low this month. Avoid scheduling important activities for now. Do as little as possible and avoid taking risks. You are more physically vulnerable, so avoid dangerous sports and other physically demanding activities. Don't engage in arguments with anyone. The energies of the month could cause a small difference to blow up into something major. There is also threat of violence and injury, so it is definitely a good idea to be careful. Listen to your instincts; if something does not feel right, back off. Otherwise the outcome will not turn out good.

### WORK & CAREER – *Stick By The Rules*

You may have to get your defenses up this month, as there are rivals disguised as friends at the workplace. Try to maintain regular contact with the top or you'll make it easy for work rivals to carry tales about you to the boss. Avoid stress by scheduling yourself enough leisure time outside of work. Learn to shut out snide remarks from covetous colleagues. Try not to break any rules this month; don't come late or leave early too often. Even if it's understood you're in a flexi-arrangement, this month it may be frowned upon. And while your superiors may not mind, your peers may be all too eager to use it against you, making it difficult for those on your side to back you up. Put the relevant feng shui symbols in place to protect against office politics and help in your pursuit of career excellence. Work smart this month and leave no room for error.

## BUSINESS – *Stay Well Informed*

Take caution when it comes to business this month. Be alert to any changes of mood and scenery. Don't follow your instincts alone when making decisions. Be as well informed as you can so you can use logic and common

Display a Rooster in the office to quell office politics.

sense when deciding on important issues. You may have a lot you want to say right now, but this is not the time to speak out. Keep grievances to yourself. If you have anything radical to propose, hold out for now. Keeping the status quo is the best way to maintain your luck through this patchy month. This is not a bad month for non-financial pursuits. Focus on the spiritual rather than the material for now.

## LOVE & RELATIONSHIPS – *Quarrelsome*

Love luck is in the doldrums. Unnecessary quarrels lead to bigger issues if you don't nip them in the bud. Change the subject or back down, but don't fight. Fighting this month could do permanent damage to your relationship.

Single Boars may be left single for a while longer. You're unlikely to find true love in a month full of antagonistic stars. If you've spotted someone who piques your interest, it may be a good idea to wait till next month before making your move. Romantic endeavors will bring much more fulfillment next month when your luck improves. For now, concentrate on looking inward to yourself and improving your skills and talents.

# 9TH MONTH
## Oct 8th - Nov 6th 2010

### ROMANCE BLOSSOMS
### FOR THOSE WHO ARE SINGLE

This is a good month for Boars looking for love and romance. For those of you who are single, you may well find the real thing this month. There is marriage on the cards or a serious relationship that could lead to marriage in the future. There is much to smile about this period! Married Boars see their love lives get a boost. Scholars benefit as their work receives recognition. Those of you in creative work will find inspiration comes easily to you. This is a good month to propose and to take relationships to the next level.

### WORK & CAREER – *Opportunities Open Up*

Career luck looks good this month and your thoughts are set beyond the here and now. You may be offered some big opportunities at work, but this may involve a change in lifestyle. You may be asked to move city or even country, or less drastically, you may be asked to take on a new position in which you have little knowledge or experience. But because your luck is good, you're likely to be able to handle anything. Be

ambitious and courageous when making decisions.
Go with your own instincts rather than let others
influence you. You know what you want and your
own judgment is what will serve you best right now.

## BUSINESS – *New Avenues to Explore*
There are many avenues for you to explore this
month. You have plenty of good ideas waiting to be
implemented. You can't pursue all of them at once,
but this month you have ally luck, and partners with
great potential could materialize offering you ways
to expand with less capital and less risk on your
part. Effective delegation will also free yourself up
to spend more time on the strategic aspects of your
business. You have some good staff on your hands and
if you need some new hires, go ahead. This is a good
period for expansion.

## LOVE & RELATIONSHIPS – *Strengthening Bonds*
This is a great month when it comes matters of the
heart. This is a time when your relationship with your
partner can grow deeper and more meaningful. If you
have been married or together a long time, it may
surprise you that there's still so much to learn about
each other. This will strengthen your bond and bring
back excitement into the relationship. Think about
taking a romantic trip away somewhere. Make use
of the loving energies of the month. It will be time

and money well spent. For Boars who are single, the sooner you're with someone, the more satisfied you'll be. You need a partner this month. Even if it's a short term partner. You might feel an acute loneliness if you don't have someone to call your own. The good news is that you're looking and feeling attractive and finding a mate is no problem.

## EDUCATION – *Great Study Luck*

Everything goes well for the student Boar this month. Your ability to retain new knowledge is high and study luck is excellent. Use this time to make the most of this kind of luck by giving more attention to your schoolwork. Whatever way you choose to study, you'll find yourself more highly motivated this month. Producing good work becomes easy when you set your mind to it. Avoid rushing assignments if you want to benefit fully from the favorable stars this month. Put effort into your work and the results will more than reflect the effort.

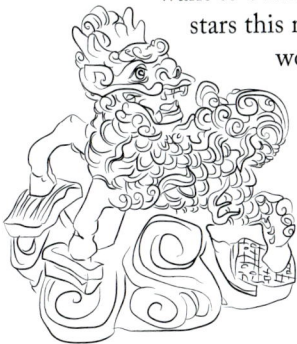

Enhance excellent study luck this month with a Chi Lin with 4 scholastic objects. Place on your study table.

# 10TH MONTH
## Nov 7th - Dec 6th 2010

### LUCK SOARS BUT
### YOU ARE ON A SHORT FUSE

There is both good and bad luck indicated in your chart. Bad luck comes in the form of arguments, quarrels and even lawsuits. You find yourself more short-tempered than usual and people around you irk you more. Watch your words as you have the knack of saying the wrong thing. Avoid being offensive or you could make some powerful enemies. Be especially careful you don't offend the wrong people when it comes to work. If you have any harsh words, keep them to yourself. Avoid indulging in gossip as it will definitely backfire this month. The good news is there is completion luck this month; projects can get finished and you can get paid. But don't let your short temper spoil your successes this month.

### WORK & CAREER – *Keep Your Cool*

Career luck is generally good this month. You can prevail over the competition if you keep your cool. Your hot blood this month will keep you efficient and on-the-ball, but it could also make you a right nuisance. Try and channel your dominant energy to producing good work. But keep in mind that your mouth is probably not your best asset this month. When engaging in group discussion, be aware of the tone you use when you contribute. There are always two ways to say the same thing. Try the tactful way and you will find that works better.

## BUSINESS – *Use Subtle Strategies*

Success is possible as long as disagreements over peripheral issues don't cloud the matters at hand. Keep discussions to the point, and don't become too personal when it comes to doing business. There is indication of much fiercer competition than you are used to on the horizon. Armed with the knowledge you have good fortune luck this month, you can be confident when making your moves. Avoid open fighting or all-out war. Be subtle with your strategies to fight back. If you use intelligence rather than anger to retaliate, you have the luck to emerge victorious.

## LOVE & RELATIONSHIPS – *Empathize*

A confrontation of a serious nature with a loved one is eminently possible this month. At first it may seem a relationship breaker, but before you start dishing out ultimatums, try to empathize with your partner, because misunderstandings are rife in months when your luck is this way. You're being plagued by the fighting star, which already predicts you will be at everyone's throats. Sweep your quarrels under the carper for now and revisit them when you're in a better frame of mind to cope.

## FRIENDSHIPS —*A Prickly Time*

Friendships go through the same chaos this month. Your friends may find you difficult to be around because of your obstinate nature. You could also misread their intentions, making them wary of sharing just about everything with you. It may be best to go into a retreat of sorts, and reemerge next month when your luck is better. Keep conversations simple and avoid contentious issues, which will almost guarantee a fight. Wear the color red to control the afflicted energy in your chart, and carry a **Wor Peng amulet** to promote peace and harmony in your relationships.

## EDUCATION — *Could Be Stressful*

If you're the ambitious kind, you could find it a stressful month especially if you are facing important exams in the near future. Make time to relax. It may seem unfair when certain assignments you hand in are unfairly marked. But sometimes you've just got to learn to live with what you've got. Look on the bright side of things and you won't feel so bad.

# 11TH MONTH
## Dec 7th - Jan 5th 2011

### WATCH WHAT YOU EAT & SLEEP EARLY THIS MONTH

You're plagued with ill health and poor resistance this month. You are also at risk of injury from accidents. Take extra care of yourself. Physical injuries such as pulled muscles and bruises may befall you. Avoid taking risks if you are involved in extreme sports. The good news is that mentally, your mind is far clearer this month and you become more at peace with yourself. Relationship luck improves and you become more popular within your social circles. Luck in love is also better. Wealth luck is average, so try not to overspend. You may have a big cheque to write in the near future and you want to be comfortable when doing so.

### WORK & CAREER – *Deadlines to Meet*

Your energy levels are down and increased work demands could catch you off guard. A project you've been working on could end up taking more time than you planned for and deadlines come down hard on you. Instead of working yourself into a panic, call on help if you can. If you're working in a team, a synchronized group effort will do the trick. But if you're working on your own, devise a plan to complete successfully. You may have to pause to plan your time, but doing so will be far more effective than trudging on relentless.

## BUSINESS – *Time to Consolidate*

Wealth luck is very average, so this is a time to consolidate rather than expand. You are not working at your best, so ensure you have a good team working with you. Trying to do everything yourself just won't work. This is also a good chance to let others prove their worth to you. You'll be surprised how productive you can be if you learn how to manage rather than do everything yourself.

You may be torn between too many people trying to advise you. If in doubt, go with your own instincts, although make time for the people you feel more comfortable with. Family and friends who have known you longer may be able to give you a more objective view of things without an ulterior motive.

## LOVE & RELATIONSHIPS – *Future Plans*

Love luck is promising and if you're single, you could soon meet someone to occupy all your thoughts. Don't be surprised if you find yourself caught up in a whirlwind romance. When it happens, it will be just the two of you and nothing else will matter! If you're ready for that kind of relationship, you could find true happiness this month. To activate for this kind of luck, wear the **double happiness symbol,** and place you **Peach Blossom Animal,** the Rat in the North corner of your bedroom.

## SCHOOL & EDUCATION – *Get Motivated*

Motivation is the key to your success this month. You have plenty of ability; you just need to want to do it. Set yourself some goals so you have something clear to work towards. But set targets that are high enough. Have some immediate goals as well as some medium term, then long term ones. Once you achieve your first goal, you'll be on a roll!

Activate for excellent love luck this month with the double happiness symbol.

# 12TH MONTH
## Jan 6th - Feb 3rd 2011

### GOOD TIME TO PLAN
### & ANALYZE YOUR SITUATION

This is a fabulous month for the Boar! The stars in your chart are aligned in your favor and many opportunities come your way. You are in your element, so make the most of this lucky time. You enjoy the sum-of-ten in your chart once again, which predicts good fortune outcomes for your projects and anything you're involved with. Stay focused if you want to reap big rewards. Business luck is good and career luck is excellent. Use this month to go after your dreams and anything you want to achieve, because this month, anything is possible! Enjoy the end of the Tiger Year. Happily for the Boar person, the coming Rabbit Year also holds out the promise of good things!

## WORK & CAREER — *Future Plans*

This month you enjoy plenty of good fortune luck and those of you focused on your career will do extremely well. Positive thinking promises to bring good results, so make sure you stay single-minded about your goals. The energies of the month also make it a good time for planning for the future. This is a time when you can lay the groundwork for later on. Strategic thinking brings particular benefits this month. The more you use your mind in your job, the better you will do. Continue setting achievable goals for yourself. Your colleagues are loyal to you this month; they will be thankful for your highly organized work style and recognize when your work ethics brings benefits to them as well.

## BUSINESS – *Winning Formula*
If there's something you are good at this month, it's finding the winning formula and managing a winning team. If you're the boss and running your own business, you'll find it easy to convey your strategies and work style to those working for you. It is easy for you to think through problems and get them solved in no time. Competition may heat up this month and grabbing your rightful share of the market may become more challenging, but it is nothing you can't cope with once you put your mind to it.

## LOVE & RELATIONSHIPS – *Changing Priorities*
If you're in a steady relationship, your connection with your partner grows stronger in the next four weeks. Your priorities when it comes to love and romance go through a change this month, and you are likely to start thinking more long-term. Some of

you may be thinking of settling down. If you feel you have met the right person, by all means go ahead. The chi energies of this month are extremely auspicious for the Boar person. The sum-of-ten in your chart brings completion luck, assuring you that deals sealed this period will last.

Those of you already married however may meet some resistance with their spouse this month, especially if both of you want to dominate the relationship. You need to work out a system of give and take. Once you do, the energies of the month become magical and you can start to enjoy one another once again.

## SCHOOL & EDUCATION – *Victory Luck*

Study luck goes well for the young Boar this month. Those of you sitting exams are likely to do very well. If you're aiming for a scholarship or award, chances of your getting it are very high. Research whatever you're targeting for carefully. If you put your heart and soul into something, you'll get it. You enjoy victory luck this month and can emerge triumphant if you keep your mind positive and focused. Place a Victory Banner in the NW of your study room this month to activate this kind of luck.

# Part 4
# Updating House Feng Shui

It is important to maintain the good feng shui of your home. For this reason as well as to ensure a smooth transition into the New Year, you should take note of time dimension feng shui which means making the vital changes necessary to ensure the New Year brings both protection and good fortune, something that is quite important for those of you born in the years of the Boar because this coming year holds some special luck for you and it is definitely advisable to make a real effort to ensure that nothing spoils the good opportunities coming your way.

This means making some changes to the placement of decorative objects and symbolic cures, making alterations to the way furniture is arranged in the public areas of your home and perhaps making some adjustments to room usage in your home. Making changes to accommodate the annual chi energy pattern is important for maintaining a balance of good energy in the home. This is what will help ensure that your good fortune for the year does not get compromised and that you are strongly protected from getting hit by nasty surprises and misfortune happenings.

This is something not many people are aware of, as a result of which even when a home has been very well designed according to feng shui principles, when no effort is made to accommodate yearly changes of energy, sometimes bad luck descends unexpectedly causing problems to suddenly descend on the family.

Usually, misfortune brought by afflictive flying stars can be severe enough to cause a high degree of stress and tribulations. In fact, when unlucky energy inadvertently flies into the part of your home where your **main door** is located, or where your **bedroom** is sited, you and your family risk being hit by some misfortune luck. This is true even when your personal horoscope chart shows your luck is good for the year.

Misfortune can manifest as a sudden illness, an unexpected accident or loss, a court case or a significant reversal of fortune that brings hardship. It is advisable then to anticipate this kind of problem, address it and then install remedies and cures. This is the best way to practice feng shui with great effectiveness.

The location and severity of **feng shui afflictions** that bring bad luck to residents in any building are revealed by annual flying stars. These are numbers that move around a specially constructed feng shui chart based on an ancient formula that maps out the changing chi movements of each New Year.

These changes alter the luck patterns of all buildings every New Year. Attending to it is part of the time aspects of feng shui practice. It is something that should be incorporated into an annual renewal of chi program for the home. Attending to this renewal process ensures that the energy of your abodes stay fresh and vigorous.

# Yearly Feng Shui Afflictions

These bring negative luck, causing misfortune, accidents, loss and a variety of ills to manifest. This Part of the book explains the severity and location of the different afflictions in the Year of the Tiger. Once you know what and where the afflictions are, it is not difficult to deal with them using element cures and other powerful traditional feng shui methods.

It is important to subdue annual feng shui afflictions because these have the potential to create havoc in your life. Misfortune can come in a variety of ways. Sometimes they manifest as severe illness suffered by some member of the family; or they can cause loss of wealth, loss of good name or loss of a loved one.

It is not difficult to control feng shui afflictions and doing so helps prevent bad luck from occurring, so everyone should really take the trouble to do so. It is worthwhile making the effort, because for most part, the remedies involve little effort.

In the past, this aspect of feng shui practice was simply ignored by modern day practitioners, leaving many vulnerable to reversals of fortune although in recent years, awareness of time dimension feng shui has increased substantially. Master practitioners of feng shui in Asia and around the world now go to great lengths to study, analyze and deal with time related feng shui afflictions at the start of each New Year.

The cut off date when energy patterns change, occur around February 4th, which is regarded as the first day of Spring – in Chinese known as the *lap chun*. This is not to be confused with the lunar New Year date which is determined by the Chinese lunar calendar. The Chinese use their solar calendar (known as the *Hsia Calendar*) to track feng shui energy changes. The monthly change of energy patterns in Part 3 of the book, for instance, uses the Hsia calendar to determine the dates when each month starts.

The feng shui chart of any year is usually depicted in a 9 x 9 sector Lo Shu square with a number in each grid. These numbers are determined by the ruling or center number which in 2010 is 8. Once the center number is known, the rest of the numbers in the different grids of square can be determined.

The numbers 1 through 9 in each of the 9 grids of the Lo Shu Square offer insights into the way the pattern of luck has moved in any built up structure or building. This investigation precedes the updating of feng shui.

In addition to afflictions, the chart also reveals the good luck sectors - i.e. those parts of your house that enjoy the most auspicious luck during the year. If the lucky numbers fly into the sector that houses your main door or bedroom, or into any part of the home where you spend a considerable amount of time, then the good energy of that location will shower you with good fortune.

Sometimes the feng shui of your bedroom can be so good it can override any kind of low energy you may be suffering from in your horoscope for the year. When auspicious numbers enter into the location of your animal sign, it will benefit you for that year. Hence understanding the annual chart feng shui enables you to subdue bad luck and bad feng shui; and to enhance good luck and good feng shui.

**When feng shui afflictions of your living and work spaces are treated with feng shui cures, and the lucky sectors are activated with auspicious decorative objects or celestial creatures, your luck for the year is sure to instantly improve.**

You can overcome obstacles to success more effectively, and make better decisions by tracking your luck through each month of the year. Timing plays a crucial role in the success factor and when armed with prior knowledge of good and bad months, you are certain to have a positive competitive edge.Updating your feng shui brings powerful benefits as you will know exactly how to be protected against sudden/major changes of fortunes. Those unprotected are vulnerable not only to annual afflictions but also to monthly ill winds that might be blowing your way. It is so important then to know about good and bad months.

Misfortune usually comes suddenly, descending on you when least expected. It can come as illness, or manifest as court action, or worse, as some kind of personal loss. Misfortune can hit at anytime. Don't think that bad things do not happen to good people, because they do. Since it requires so little effort to guard against bad luck and bad feng shui, it seems foolish not to do so.

## Luck of Different Parts of the Home

The annual feng shui chart reveals the luck of every part of the house categorized into compass sectors. So every corner of the home must be investigated. Each sector has a number from 1 through 9, and there are eight outer sectors plus the center. In 2010 the center sector ruling number is 8. The remaining numbers are identified once the center number is known.

## 2010 Annual Feng Shui Chart

| SE | S | SW |
|---|---|---|
| 7 | 3 | 5 |
| 6 | **8** | 1 |
| 2 | 4 | 9 |
| NE | N | NW |

| E | | W |

The numbers in this chart change or "fly" from year to year, reflecting changes in energy in the different direction sectors. Each of the numbers in the different compass locations reveals the quality of energy ruling that location in 2010.

These numbers enable a knowledgeable feng shui practitioner to instantly identify afflicted sectors. These are the parts of the house where remedies need to be put in place to suppress the afflictions. Doing so - subduing the afflictions of the different parts of the house - brings protection to the whole house!

In the same way, the luckiest sectors can also be ascertained and then activated to manifest good luck. When individual sectors get enhanced the improved, chi energy spreads to the rest of the house. It is vital to study the feng shui chart for 2010 which is done in this book. Then you, the reader can superimpose it onto the layout sketches of your home. You should use a good compass to identify the compass locations of your home.

Familiarize yourself with the chart of 2010 and systematically list down the afflictions that are particularly harmful for your house. Remember that when bad luck numbers occur in rooms that you or your family use often, that is when placing the correct remedies and cures take on some urgency. If the bad luck numbers fall into store rooms, toilets, kitchens or better yet, to parts of house that make up missing corners, then the misfortune bringing numbers should have little negative effect.

When these bad luck numbers come into your bedroom, or afflict important doors and areas of the home (such as the dining area and family area) then once again remedies become very important.

The same analogy applies to good luck stars. When these fly into important and heavy traffic rooms, the auspicious luck gets activated, and they then bring benefits to residents; and when they enter into small rooms like store rooms or tight little alcoves in the home, their good effect does not benefit the household as much.

# Activating Good Star Numbers

You need to remember that in flying star feng shui, good and bad luck numbers need to be activated either by placing an object that symbolizes a producing element (such as Water element producing Wood element in a Wood sector like East or SE) or with an auspicious decorative item. Here, knowing what **celestial creature** to display and what **element** is favorable for the year will help you to vastly improve your feng shui.

Other ways to activate good numbers is to increase the level of yang energy in the corners benefiting from the year's good fortune numbers. Thus using bright lights and increasing sound levels in the center of the house in 2010, for example, should benefit the household greatly. This is because the center plays host to the auspicious 8 and activating it is sure to bring benefits.

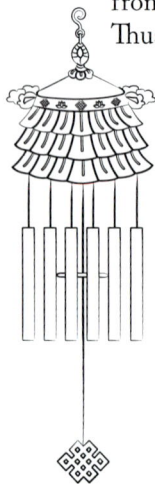

Hang the victor banner windchime in the center of the home to activate the lucky number 8 this year.

In 2010, the center of the home should be energized by the presence of **multiple crystal balls** – eight should be an excellent number. This strengthens the Earth element of the center and since 8 is itself an Earth element number, and considering that the earth element symbolizes wealth in 2010, enhancing Earth energy is excellent indeed. Crystal balls of any kind will be very beneficial for the center of the home in 2010.

The large **Tara Crystal Ball** which we brought out last year to energize 8 in the SE sector then was a great success for many people and for those who want to use these again in 2010, just move it to the center of the room. Make sure you twirl it daily because this activates the positive effects of crystal ball; as the ball contains the praises to the Goddess Tara, twirling the ball activates its wish-fulfilling aspect.

There is also another crystal ball which contains the powerful six syllable *Om Mani Padme Hum* mantra in Tibetan. For those wanting to create an aura of blessings in the home you can also place this **Om Mani Crystal Ball** in the center of the home, or on the coffee table in the living room. A golden 8 embedded inside the crystal ball activates the power of 8.

To make the feng shui even more effective, make sure you keep the light turned on as much as possible in the center of the home as fire enhances earth. Light combined with the action of twirling the ball ensures that good positive yang energy gets generated. This draws auspicious energy into the home. We have also designed a beautiful **Crystal 8** with real gold flakes embedded within to be placed in the center of the home. This will add significantly to the enhancement of the Earth element which will be so beneficial in 2010. Another powerful enhancer which can be placed in the center of the home to activate the auspicious 8 are the **Victory Banner Windchimes**.

Crystal 8 with gold specks embedded inside for the center of the living room.

# Feng Shui Chart of 2010

The feng shui chart of 2010 is created by placing the ruling number of the year in the center. We have already taken note that the ruling number of the year is 8, and considering that we are currently in the period of 8, this makes the number 8 extremely significant and very lucky indeed this year.

## 2010 Year of the Golden Tiger

The feng shui chart and 24 Mountain Stars of the Golden Tiger Year 2010.

Activating the 8 in the center brings amazing good fortune and this is the reason why we are strongly recommending the **crystal 8 with gold** for the center of the house!

Those whose Kua number or Lo Shu number is 8 can expect the year to go well for them, as this is also the period of 8. Just make sure you make an effort to activate the 8 in the center of the house. Those whose Kua number is 8 will benefit the most and this also includes women whose Kua number is 5. This is because Kua number 5 transforms to 8 for women.

You can check the Lo Shu and Kua numbers of your loved ones and friends from the resource tables contained in our *Feng Shui Diary 2010*, specially designed for the Year of the Tiger.

The feng shui chart of the year can be used to study the feng shui of any building, but you must use a compass to get your bearings and to anchor the directions of the different rooms of your house or office. Then systematically investigate the luck of every sector.

# Luck Stars of the 24 Mountains

In addition to numbers of the chart, we also study the influences of the stars that fly into the 24 mountain directions of the compass. These "stars" do not carry the same weighting in terms of their strength and luck-bringing potential, but they add important nuances to annual chart readings, and are extracted from the Almanac. Incorporating the influence of the stars adds depth to a reading of the year's feng shui energy, and for each of the twelve signs.

Together, the stars and the numbers reveal accurate and significant things about the year, and when we add the influence of the year's elements, readings for each of the animal signs become very potent and exciting. This assists you to get the best from the year. The seamless merging of Chinese Zodiac Astrology with feng shui comprise the core strength and great value of our little astrology books which we take great joy and pride in researching and writing every year.

This is the seventh year of our *Fortune & Feng Shui* list. Each year we delve a little deeper into all that influences the fortune and luck of the twelve animal signs, and the feng shui recommendations contained herein take account of these influences. Please use the analysis in this section to move from sector to sector and from room to room in your home, systematically installing feng shui remedies affected by bad chi energy. Place powerful decorative energizers and protective images to create and safeguard good luck.

# ILLNESS STAR 2
## Hits the Northeast in 2010

| SE | S | SW |
|:--:|:-:|:--:|
| 7 | 3 | 5 |
| 6 | 8 | 1 |
| 2 | 4 | 9 |
| NE | N | NW |

(E is on the left side, W on the right side)

This is the Illness Star which flies to NE in 2010. The "star" brings propensity to getting sick for those whose bedroom or door is located in the NE sector of the home.

The illness star 2 flies to the NE in 2010. This is an Earth element sector and since the illness star 2 is an Earth element number, it makes the illness affliction extremely strong in the Year of the Tiger. Earth flying into Earth suggests that those residing in the NE of their homes, or having an office or a front door in the NE tend to be vulnerable to getting sick. Unless the illness-bringing energy in this part of buildings - homes and offices - **gets strongly suppressed**, people residing or working in that part of the building are likely to develop physical ailments. And since the illness star is strong this year, it is harder to control.

If your bedroom is located in the NE sector of your house, you must make sure that suitable remedies are placed in your bedroom to suppress illness vibes.

When the main door of the house is located in the NE, the constant opening and closing of the door is sure to activate the illness-bringing star. It is advisable to try and use another door located in another sector. If this is not possible then try exhausting the Earth energy here.

Remove all Earth element items such as crystals, porcelain vases or stone objects. Also keep lights here dim to reduce Fire element energy. This is because Fire element strengthens Earth element.

Place a Wu Lou in the NE this year as a cure against the illness star.

## Cures for the Illness Star of 2010

There are excellent remedies that can be used to suppress the illness star. In 2010, a **Tiger/Dragon Wu Lou** would be especially effective. Another excellent cure is the powerful **Antahkarana Symbol** which is powerful enough to suppress the strong illness star this year, especially when it is made of metal. Brass is especially good as Metal exhausts the Earth energy of the illness star.

The symbol itself is a powerful symbol of healing and has a three-dimensional effect that cuts directly into harmful negative energy. Get this symbol and place under the bed if your bed is located in the NE of your bedroom, or if your bedroom itself is in the NE. Sleep with the symbol of the Antahkarana under your pillow, or better yet, wear the Antakahrana ring preferably made in yellow gold. The energies emitted by the powerful Antahkarana symbol – a trinity of 7 placed inside a circle - will effectively keep sickness at bay.

The healing symbol of Antahkarana.

# LITIGATION STAR 3
## Hits the South in 2010

| SE | S | SW |
|:--:|:--:|:--:|
| 7 | **3** | 5 |
| 6 | 8 | 1 |
| 2 | 4 | 9 |
| NE | N | NW |

(E on left side, W on right side)

This is the unlucky 3 Star which brings court cases & quarrels. It flies to the South in 2010, affecting all of you whose room or office is located in the South. Use red or fire energy to suppress.

The noisy, quarrelsome star 3, which brings the aggravating energy of litigation and court cases, flies to the South part of homes and offices in 2010. This star brings an air of hostility and creates a variety of problems associated with arguments, fights and misunderstandings to everyone directly hit by it. In extreme cases, when this Wood element star is enhanced, the quarrelling can lead to court cases and even violence for residents spending time in the South. The number 3 star can cause a host of interpersonal strife to flare up even between the closest of allies, friends and loved ones. It causes tempers to fray and usually manifests in a great deal of impatience.

Fortunately for anyone with a bedroom in the South, the quarrelsome star 3 is less strong this year because its intrinsic Wood element is exhausted by the Fire energy of the South. The 3 Star is a Wood element star and the traditional way of overcoming this is to exhaust it with Fire element energy. Anything that suggests Fire is an excellent cure, so all kinds of lights and the color red are suitable remedies. Hence because the South is so strongly associated with Fire energy, the sector itself has its own in-built remedy!

The Fire Sword symbolizes Metal & Fire energy - this is one of the best remedies to subdue Star 3. Place in the South in 2010.

## Earth Seal in the South

A good indication for the South location in 2010 is that the sector benefits from the presence of the **Earth Seal** brought by the luck star of the 24 mountains; this brings good fortune to those residing in this part of the house, especially if you take action to enhance this energy with Earth element activators such as **solid crystal** or **glass globes**.

Houses that face South should place the **Fire Sword** here as a safeguard against being hauled into court or getting involved in a tiresome legal battle perhaps left over from past years.

Should you be already involved in litigation, or find yourself in a prolonged battle with someone or some company, the number 3 star will hurt you if you have a bedroom in the South or if your house is facing South. If this is the case with you, do use **strong bright lights** to help you overcome it.

A dramatic remedy which brings some relief from aggravation is simply to paint the South part of the house **a bright red** – perhaps a wall or a door if this is the front part of the home.

# MISFORTUNE STAR 5
## Hits the Southwest in 2010

| SE | S | SW |
|----|----|----|
| 7 | 3 | 5 |
| 6 | 8 | 1 |
| 2 | 4 | 9 |
| NE | N | NW |

E — W

The Five Yellow Star, flies to the SW hurting the matriarchal energy of every home. This is a serious affliction which must be suppressed with the 5 element pagoda with "Hum" empowering syllable.

The Five Yellow star, also known as the *wu wang* flies to the SW in 2010 making it a very serious affliction this year. This is a star to be feared as it brings aggravations, misfortunes and most of all in 2010, a big weakness to the Matriarch of the family.

This is because SW is usually associated with the mother energy of any home, and in feng shui, when the matriarchal energy gets afflicted, it usually has a strong impact on the rest of the family as well. This is because SW is the source of the family's nurturing chi. As we are currently in the period of

8, the SW/NE directional axis exerts a great deal of strong chi for any home and when the energy of this axis brings misfortune, it must be firmly subdued. In 2010 this axis direction appears to be powerfully afflicted, with Five Yellow (*wu wang*) in the SW and 2 in the NE.

The *wu wang* is very dangerous in normal years, but in 2010, it is extremely strong as it is an Earth star flying into an Earth sector. Likewise, the illness star 2 in the NE is also strong! The *wu wang* thus gets strengthened, as a result of which, it can create havoc for mothers and also for other older women of the household.

Those having their bedroom here will also feel its negative impact and when a house faces SW, the *wu wang* can bring misfortunes that affect the entire household of residents. If there is a door in the SW that you frequently use, the *wu wang* gets activated, and this further compounds its strength. So, it is advisable to use another door if possible. The opening and closing of doors activates the energy around it.

Everyone must suppress the pernicious effects of this number 5 star – otherwise its negative influence can spread to other parts of the house. It must be strongly curbed with powerful metallic and symbolic remedies. These should best be prominently placed, on a table or sideboard in the SW of the house and office as well as in the SW of afflicted bedrooms and living rooms.

## Cures for the Wu Wang

For 2010, we recommend three powerful cures for this affliction. These should be used together for fast and powerful results. The remedies are:

1) **Five Element Pagoda with Ten Powerful Mantras**

This year, this traditional remedy comes with a larger base and the powerful mantras are stamped all round the base of the pagoda. This version of the five element pagoda is recommended for use in larger rooms and is best when placed above ground, preferably on a table. The mantras on the pagoda transform it into a powerful object which should be respected, so place it on a table.

The Five Element Pagoda with Ten Powerful Mantras is recommended for larger rooms afflicted by the *wu wang* star.

## 2) The Five Element Big Bell

This cure is best when 12 inches high. The bell is divided into 5 horizontal sections, each one signifying the 5 elements. Powerful Sanskrit mantras are embossed on its outside so that each time the bell is struck, it subdues the *wu wang* or Five Yellow affliction.

Here the sound of metal struck on metal is what suppresses the negative influences of the five yellow. Strike the bell at least once a day and more often if residents are going through a hard time. The sound of the bell with the resonance of the mantras is very powerful for dispelling bad vibes. All misfortune luck gets alleviated instantly. This is the most powerful cure against the Five Yellow. If you prefer you can use the **ringing bell** instead and the way to suppress the *wu wang* is to ring this bell around the home each day.

Strike the bell at least once a day to suppress the negative influences of the 5 Yellow in the SW.

### 3) **Double Circle Pendant**

If you want to ensure continuous suppression of any ongoing misfortune luck or if you or your family are going through really tough times associated with broken relationships and loss of income (such as losing your job) it is beneficial for members of the family to wear the Double Circle pendant. This will activate powerful Metal energy to exhaust the effects of the *wu wang*.

Better yet if the pendant has multiple circles and in the center there is a square design. This indicates the *wu wang* is kept under control.

Please note that unless suppressed, the *wu wang* brings severe illness, accidents and loss that occur in many aspects of life. It is the catalyst for bringing all kinds of misfortunes. It can cause your life to suddenly collapse around you without warning.

When you read about tragedies striking a family, you can be sure that the Five Yellow is somehow responsible, either because it afflicts the main door or the room the person occupies. Sometimes, just facing the *wu wang* direction can bring some kind of bad luck.

If your main door, your bedroom or even your office desk is afflicted by the *wu wang*, the affliction must be dealt with before the 4th February 2010. Do not be careless or forget about it as bad luck can manifest quickly. When it does it might be too late to do something about it. Prevention is better than cure, so do not wait until it is too late.

Those living in SW-facing houses should take note of the months when you need to be extra careful of the Five Yellow. We stress this because it is a serious feng shui affliction in 2010.

**As a person born in the Boar year, you must be extra careful in the month of September, as is when the *wu wang* flies into your month chart. This is when you are subjected to a double whammy of bad luck so do be careful.**

Misfortunes caused by the Five Yellow can be severe business loss or threatening terminal illness. Houses that face the SW require one or all 3 of the remedies suggested. This is because houses that face SW are sitting NE which is being hit by the illness star. Metal energy works well here at both the front and back of the house. If you reside in a room located in the SW, your cures should be inside your room. Make sure that cures are in place from February 4th, the start of the Chinese solar year!

While remedies used in previous years can be recycled after they have been cleansed with salt, it is better to retire them by throwing them into the sea or a fast moving river. It is always better to use new products with fresh new energy.

New remedies are better for suppressing feng shui afflictions, as the energy of new objects are more vigorous and thus more effective.

## Observe the "NO RENOVATION RULE" for the Southwest in 2010

It is extremely harmful if you were to undertake any kind of knocking, banging or digging in the SW in 2010. This will especially hurt the mother of the household. So do observe the "No Renovation" rule for the SW during 2010.

Any kind of demolition work poses serious danger. Misfortunes are sure to manifest. It is especially dangerous to drill floors, knock down walls, dig holes in the ground, engage in any kind of destructive work or make excessive banging kind of noise.

Any of these activities have the effect of activating the *wu wang* which in turn is sure to trigger very severe misfortune luck to suddenly manifest. The way to safeguard against this is to keep the SW location of the home very quiet in 2010.

If you really have to undertake renovations in your house and it encroaches into the SW, make sure your cures are in place **AND** make very sure the renovation does not start or end in the SW.

No one should be staying in the SW sector when renovations are going on.

If you are adding to the SW however, and not disturbing the space with banging and digging, then that kind of renovation is acceptable; and can even be auspicious. But as long as you are demolishing or digging the earth/floor, it is advisable to postpone whatever you may be planning for the sector.

Do not start or end renovations works in the SW in 2010.

# ROBBERY STAR 7
## Strikes the Southeast in 2010

| SE | S | SW |
|----|---|-----|
| 7 | 3 | 5 |
| 6 | 8 | 1 |
| 2 | 4 | 9 |
| NE | N | NW |

E (left side)  W (right side)

The Robbery Star brings violence & turmoil in your life. At its worst, the 7 brings armed robbery that can cause fatal results. Protect against it with the Blue Rhino & Elephant.

This is a very unwelcome affliction that is brought by the number 7. It is a number that causes political turmoil and sparks aggressive behavior that can become something serious very fast and this is because it is the violent star. It brings out the worst in all who come under its influence or is afflicted by it. In 2010, it flies to the SE where its presence creates dangerous situations for those residing here in the SE sector. This star number completely dominates the sector because being of the Metal element, it easily controls the Wood Element of the SE. So the 7 is very lethal here.

The SE is the place of the eldest daughter so daughters should be especially careful. Anyone living in the SE should also be very careful as this star number brings danger of violence and burglary. It is advisable to try and avoid this sector.

For 2010, because the Water element is so lacking during the year, the best remedy for the SE, for the whole house to be protected from the 7 star, residents should display the special **Blue Rhino and Elephant water globe**. This is a very powerful cure for the violent burglary star. Placing or incorporating the water globe or water motif here is an excellent idea.

The good news is that in the year 2010, the Luck Stars of the 24 Mountains for the SE are extremely auspicious. Thus the *Star of the Golden Deity* which brings heaven's blessings benefits all those residing in the SE1 location. At the same time, the SE3 location is favored by the *Heavenly Seal* which also brings auspicious energy. This benefits anyone staying here.

These two powerful heavenly stars of the 24 Mountains are an excellent buffer against the annoyance of the burglary star as it is sandwiched between two powerful stars. This helps residents of the SE overcome burglary woes in 2010. Remember that the best way to overcome its negative effect of 7 is to have a large water feature as water exhausts the vitality of 7.

Water is always auspicious for the SE where it strengthens the intrinsic Wood energy here. Those who already have a water feature here such as a pond in the garden or an internal water feature in the living room will be happy to know that in addition to generating good fortune luck for the eldest daughter of the family, water here suppress the burglary star of 2010 and brings much needed Water energy for the year.

The Blue Rhino & Elephant Water Globe is a powerful cure against the burglary star 7 which flies into the SE sector this year.

# The Tai Sui Resides in the Northeast in 2010

The 2010 *Tai Sui* resides in the location of NE3 which is the home location of the Crouching Tiger; however, despite occupying the den of the Tiger, this year's Tai Sui is not wrathful, and like the Tai Sui of the previous year is not quick to anger even when disturbed or confronted.

Nevertheless, to be on the safe side, it is advisable to keep the Tai Sui appeased and happy. The best way of doing this is to place the Tai Sui plaque with a **specially written Taoist talisman**. This not only appeases the Tai Sui, it also successfully enlists the Tai Sui's help to attract prosperity and abundance.

## The Effect of the Tai Sui Affliction

If you believe in feng shui, do take the affliction of the Tai Sui seriously. This is emphasized in the Treatise on Harmonizing Times and Distinguishing Directions compiled under the patronage of the Qianlong Emperor during his reign in the mid-Eighteenth century. The Emperor placed great importance on the astrological influences on the luck of the dynasty.

He particularly stressed on the correct ways for selecting times and aligning houses and in fact went to great lengths to ensure that all knowledge on these matters were properly catalogued for posterity. The Treatise confirms that the astrology of the Tai Sui is recognized since mid century BCE (for over 2000 years) and it states that the locations where the Tai Sui resides and where the Tai Sui has just vacated are lucky locations.

So note that in 2010, the locations of NE1 and NE3 are lucky. Those having their rooms in these two locations will enjoy the patronage and protection of the Tai Sui in 2010.

The Treatise explains that it is unlucky to reside in the location where the Tai Sui is progressing towards i.e. clockwise on the astrology compass and in 2010 this means the East 2 location; it is unlucky to directly confront the Tai Sui's residence.

Place a Pi Yao in the NE in 2010 to appease the Tai Sui in 2010.

**It is unlucky to "face" the Tai Sui because this is deemed rude, so the advice for 2010 is not to directly face NE3 direction. Actually, doing so also causes you to directly confront the Tiger, and this is definitely not advisable.**

So for 2010 you must remember not to face NE3 even if this is your most favored direction under the Eight Mansions School of feng shui. When you face the Tai Sui, nothing you do will go smoothly as obstacles surface unexpectedly and friends turn into adversaries. You should also place the beautiful **Pi Yao** in the NE as this celestial chimera is incredibly auspicious and also has the power to appease the Tai Sui and to get him on your side.

**NOTE:** An important reminder for 2010 is to not disturb the place of the Tai Sui which means the NE3 location should not be renovated this year. Refrain from drilling, digging, banging and knocking down walls or digging holes in the ground. Those starting renovations in 2010 to change to a Period 8 house are advised not to start or end their renovations in NE3 and to avoid starting or ending their renovations in November when the direction of the Tai Sui is afflicted by misfortune star of *wu wang*.

# The Three Killings
# Flies to the North in 2010

In 2010 the North of every building is afflicted by the Three Killings. This feng shui aggravation affects only the primary directions, but that means its bad effects are felt over a larger area of the house - 90 degrees! This affliction brings 3 severe misfortunes associated with loss, grief and sadness. Its location each year is charted according to the animal sign that rules the year. Thus it flies to the North in 2010 because the Tiger belongs to the Triangle of Affinity made up of the Tiger, Dog and Horse and of these 3 animal signs, it is the Horse which occupies a cardinal direction (South).

The Three Killings is in the North this year, the direction that is directly opposite the Horse. The Three Killings causes three kinds of loss; the loss of one's good reputation, the loss of a loved one and the loss of wealth. When you suffer a sudden reversal of fortune, it is usually due to being hit by the Three Killings. In 2010, the Three Killings resides in the North where it poses some danger to the middle sons of the family. Anyone occupying the North will be very vulnerable to being hit by the Three Killings.

## Cures for the Three Killings

In terms of cures, we are recommending the three divine guardians - comprising the Chi Lin, the Fu Dog and the Pi Yao.

The Three Divine Guardians can be used to control the Three Killings affliction in the North in 2010.

We have been using these celestial protectors with great success for several years now and we can continue using them for 2010. It is however advisable to bring in newly minted ones to ensure their energy is fresh and there is strong vigor and vitality.

The three guardians are a great favorite with the Chinese and they create a powerful and invisible shield of protective energy that prevents the Three Killings from passing into the home or office.

**It is a good idea to keep all North sector doors and windows closed during the afternoon hours as this is an effective way of preventing the energy of the Three Killings from entering.**

Another powerful set of cures to overpower the three killings in the year of the Tiger are the **Three Deities** each sitting on a Tiger and therefore symbolizing their dominance over this powerful beast. Deities that sit on the Tiger are usually also wealth-bringing Gods. The most effective then is to line up the Wealth God sitting on a Tiger (Tsai Shen Yeh), the Eight Immortal sitting on a Tiger and one of the 18 Arhats sitting on a Tiger. The symbolism of these three powerful Deities cannot be matched and their presence in the home is also an effective way of avoiding all the difficult luck brought by the Tiger in 2010.

A Wealth God sitting on a tiger symbolizes his dominance over the animal and displaying his image in the home helps you bring the fierce energies of the Tiger Year under control.

# THE LUCKY STAR 4 bringing
## Romance & Study Luck to the North

| SE | S | SW |
|:--:|:--:|:--:|
| 7 | 3 | 5 |
| 6 | 8 | 1 |
| 2 | 4 | 9 |
| NE | N | NW |

*(E on left, W on right)*

The Lucky Star 4 flies North bringing love & romance to this part of houses in 2010. The star 4 is also beneficial for anyone engaged in writing, study and work.

The North comes out of a challenging year to play host to the romance-bringing star in 2010. Last year, the North had been afflicted by the *wu wang*, but this year this is the location which attracts love and marriage opportunities, developments of the heart brought by the peach blossom vibes here. This luck is considered good for singles and unmarried people but is viewed with suspicion for those who are already married. *Peach blossom luck* is usually linked to temptations of the heart and to unfaithful behavior for the older married. As such, this is not a star favored by those already married. So if your room is in the North part of the house and you are already married, it is not a bad idea to symbolically suppress it with **bright lights** or Fire element energy.

This should prevent either husband or wife succumbing to temptation coming their way. Placing an **amethyst geode tied with red string** and attached to the bed is a Taoist way of keeping the marriage stable, and spouses faithful.

Unmarried people who want to activate their marriage luck can do so with the presence of all the marriage symbols such as the **dragon and phoenix,** and the **double happiness character**. Here in the North, the romance star favors young men who are still single. So those of you keen on enhancing marriage luck should activate your peach blossom luck by placing a **Bejeweled Rat** in the North. However, note that the Chinese usually do not favor romance blossoming in a Tiger Year and they usually wait until the following Year of the Rabbit before committing themselves in a new love relationship.

The double happiness symbol is ideal for attracting marriage luck. It should be worn or incorporated into house or room decor for best results.

## Scholastic Luck

Those residing in the North part of the house will also enjoy the other influences brought by the same number 4 star which are also related to scholastic and literary pursuits.

The number 4's literary side is strong, bringing academic luck to those residing in this part of the home. Those facing North will also benefit from this powerful star of learning and is especially suitable for students and those sitting for examinations.

> **The direction North stands for career luck so this auspicious number is a very positive star here. The only problem will be that love can also be a distraction, so if you want to enhance the scholastic side of this star, you should place literary symbols here.**

The number 4 benefits those engaged in writing and literary careers. Those employed in a writing career or in the media or are involved in any kind of academic pursuits benefit from staying in the North. Enhancing this part of the house is sure to bring benefits.

Feng shui energizers for the North in 2010 are categorized into those benefiting the romance side and those wanting to activate the scholastic side. For love and romance, place **mandarin ducks** here and better yet, hang a **love mirror** to reflect in the energies of the cosmic universe from outside. Meanwhile those wanting to jump start their scholastic or literary pursuits should look for a good specimen of a **single-pointed quartz crystal** and then write a powerful wishfulfilling mantra on it. This is an excellent way of helping you to improve your concentration and your studies.

Write a wishfulfilling mantra on a single-pointed natural quartz crystal to help you in your studies.

# WHITE STAR 1 brings
## Triumphant Success to the West

| SE | S | SW |
|---|---|---|
| 7 | 3 | 5 |
| 6 | 8 | 1 |
| 2 | 4 | 9 |

(E on left side, W on right side; NE, N, NW along bottom)

The Victory Star is in the West - it is flanked by the 2 "Big Auspicious" stars of the 24 mountains. This makes the West sector extremely lucky in 2010 and those having rooms here can take advantage of this.

Those residing in rooms in the West corner of your house will benefit from the white star of victory, the number 1 star which brings triumph and success in 2010. This star number helps you to win in any competitive situation.

It is the star that brings triumphant luck helping anyone receiving its chi energy to emerge successfully in any kind of competition. The attainment of success is easier for you, especially if you also energize the number 1 star correctly and effectively. In 2010 this star brings good fortune to young women, especially the youngest daughters of families and also the youngest women in any household. However, please note that the number 1 star in 2010 is not as vigorous as it was last year. There is definitely a relative reduction in energy.

Nevertheless, the West location is regarded as being extremely auspicious in 2010 as there are two powerful Big Auspicious luck stars brought by the 24 Mountains to the West. Anyone residing in this part of the house will benefit from having the Victory Banner placed here. It is important that this be made of brass metal to strengthen the metal element of this corner. You can also wear the **Victory Banner** as a pendant made of gold.

The Victory Banner is a symbol of winning over the competition. Excellent for those in the running for a promotion.

# CELESTIAL STAR 6
## Creates Windfall Luck in the East

| SE | S | SW |
|:---:|:---:|:---:|
| 7 | 3 | 5 |
| **6** (E) | 8 | 1 (W) |
| 2 | 4 | 9 |
| NE | N | NW |

The celestial luck of 6 brings excellent news through the year. The number 6 stands for heavenly energy which unites with earth and mankind to create the trinity of Tien Ti Ren.

This is the number 6 white star which is associated with the powerful **Trigram Chien**, so its presence in the East creates the synergy luck between father and eldest son. When the bedroom of the family's eldest son is located in this sector of the house, he is certain to benefit very much from unexpected good fortune, the kind that comes without warning, and is thus a welcome surprise.

The 6 star brings heaven's celestial blessings. There is also the presence of the *Golden Deity* star which strengthens the help from heaven diagnosis for the

East. To activate this auspicious star, **welcome in a Golden Deity sitting on a Dragon** to this sector. One such deity is the White Dzambhala – the Tibetan Deity of Wealth – which sits on a Dragon and carries a gem-spouting mongoose!

In Flying Star feng shui, the number 6 signifies everything to do with the management of economics and finances. At its peak, 6 stands for authority, influence and control over money, like being the Head of a Bank.

When 6 appears in the East, the popular interpretation is that economic power does well when managed in the hands of a young man. This is also a military star which brings promotions and mentor luck.

It is incredibly beneficial to activate this auspicious star to benefit the whole household and this can be done by displaying **6 large smooth coins** in the East sector. Doing so ensures that everything will move smoothly for the household. It is also a very powerful way of attracting Mentor Luck into the household – powerful and influential friends who can and will assist you, opening doorways to opportunities for you.

The power of six metal coins should never be underestimated.

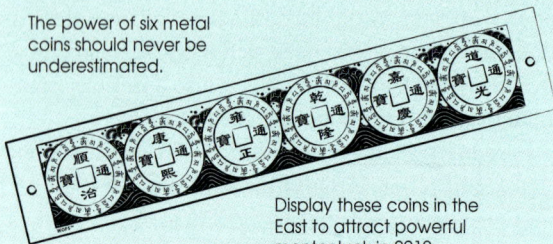

Display these coins in the East to attract powerful mentor luck in 2010.

# Updating Your Feng Shui

Updating feng shui is something that many wealthy and powerful families in places like Hong Kong, Taiwan and now China arrange for without fail each year. In recent years, the practice is also becoming increasingly popular in Singapore, Malaysia and Indonesia.

**Today, families consult feng shui retainers who use their expertise to insure homes against the intangible feng shui afflictions of the year. But these days, anyone keen to do so can update their feng shui.**

At *World of Feng Shui*, the annual feng shui chart is analyzed each year. This makes it possible for us to understand the nature and location of bad luck afflictions and good luck indications.

We explain the use of different remedies each year through our popular *Feng Shui Extravaganzas* which are whole day events held in Singapore, Malaysia, the USA, UK and in 2010, for the first time, also in French Polynesia! These events go a long way towards protecting against the year's afflictions.

The *Feng Shui Extravaganza* road show is a wonderful way to connect with feng shui enthusiasts and to explain the fine points on what needs to be done each New Year. Those interested to attend any of our 2010 Feng Shui Extravaganzas, the dates and venues can be accessed at www.wofs.com.

# Part 5
# Improving personal feng shui

Each New Year, in addition to updating your space feng shui, it also benefits to make some spatial adjustments that update your individual feng shui.

The practice of personalised feng shui takes into account your animal sign as well as your individual Kua number. You need to make adjustments to your facing directions and sitting locations to take account of the different energies of the Tiger Year; thus your lucky and unlucky directions as indicated by your Kua number must be fine-tuned to allow for the year's chi afflictions.

Remember that in using your lucky directions you must always be mindfully aware of the influences of various annual afflictions. Even when a direction is considered "lucky" for you, if in the Year of the Tiger that direction is adversely affected in any way, then you must NOT face that direction. Annual energies usually override Kua number lucky directions. Thus if your love direction is afflicted this year, then it is best not to activate romance luck this year. Personalizing your feng shui makes a big difference to improving luck, especially in a year as challenging as this one. Also, using your birth Lo Shu number to see how it combines with this year's Lo Shu number 8 offers some interesting nuances for you to work with.

## Finetuning Your Kua Lucky & Unlucky Directions

The compass-based method of using your Kua number to determine if you are East or West group, and also for finding our your lucky and unlucky directions, is one of the easiest ways to practice and benefit from compass formula feng shui. Once you know your lucky directions, all you need to do is to arrange your home and office and the furniture within in a way which enables you to always face at least one of your good luck (and unafflicted) directions. Just doing this will immediately make a difference to your luck for the year.

## Lo Shu & Kua Numbers for Boar

| Birth Year | Element BOAR | Age in 2010 | Lo Shu No. at Birth | KUA No. for Men | KUA No. for Women |
|---|---|---|---|---|---|
| 1935 | Wood Boar | 75 | 2 | 2 | 4 |
| 1947 | Fire Boar | 63 | 8 | 8 | 7 |
| 1959 | Earth Boar | 51 | 5 | 5 | 1 |
| 1971 | Metal Boar | 39 | 2 | 2 | 4 |
| 1983 | Water Boar | 27 | 8 | 8 | 7 |
| 1995 | Wood Boar | 15 | 5 | 5 | 1 |

The formula in detail identifies four different kinds of good luck and four severities of bad luck, with each being represented by a compass direction. The four good directions allows you to choose whether to face a direction that brings you success, love, good health of improves your personal growth.

The formula also identifies four kinds of misfortune directions, describing the nature and intensity of each of these bad luck directions. Once you are aware of your misfortune directions, all you need to do is to systematically change your sitting and sleeping arrangements so that you will never face or have your head pointed to any of the bad luck directions. arrangements so that you will never face or have your head pointed to any of the bad luck directions. Feng shui is really that simple!

**But there is one extra thing** you need to take account of and that is to finetune these lucky and unlucky directions.

1) Check if any of your **lucky directions** are afflicted by any of the afflictive stars of the New Year. This requires you to study the afflicted directions laid out in the previous chapter.

2) Take note of your own animal sign compass location and ensure that this location is properly activated and kept free of clutter, even if this is not one of your lucky directions. Remember that your animal sign direction is more important and also overrides the Kua directions!

Your animal sign direction (which in the case of the Boar is NW3) is always lucky for you irrespective of what the Kua formula indicates. It overrides the Kua formula, but if the direction is afflicted by a bad number star for the year, then the location and direction should be avoided. In the year of the Tiger, the NW enjoys the lucky star 9 which brings the luck of future prosperity, thus opening opportunities especially for younger Boar people establish foundations for future success.

This NW direction is lucky for West group Boar people (those with Kua numbers 2, 5, 7 and 8) but because in 2010 this sector is lucky, it is also acceptable for East group Boar people (i.e. those with Kua Numbers 1 and 4). Even if NW may be unlucky for you, using this direction in 2010 will not harm you. It is useful for you to know that the number 9 also magnifies luck whether good or bad. Hence enhancing the number 9 with a small amount of fire element energy here in the NW is a good idea even though NW is a metal sector. The Fire energy will not hurt the Metal.

3) You also need to look at your Lo Shu number at birth and see how this interacts with the Lo Shu number of the year which is 8. The Lo Shu numbers of Boar are 2, 5 or 8 all of which are Earth numbers.

You should find out whether any of your lucky directions are in any way affected by bad luck stars during the year. Every year, the direction of misfortune-bringing afflictions change, so it is

# Lucky & Unlucky Directions for Boar

| Male/Female Monkey | Male | Male | Male | Female | Female | Female |
|---|---|---|---|---|---|---|
| **Kua Number** | 2 | 5 | 8 | 1 | 4 | 7 |
| **Success Direction** | NE* | NE* | SW* | SE* | North | NW |
| **Love Direction** | NW | NW | West | South* | East | NE* |
| **Health Direction** | West | West | NW | East | South* | SW* |
| **Personal Growth** | SW* | SW* | NE* | North | SE* | West |
| **Bad Luck Direction** | East | East | South* | West | NW | North |
| **Five Ghosts Direction** | SE* | SE* | North | NE* | SW* | South* |
| **Six Killings Direction** | South* | South* | East | NW | West | SE* |
| **Total Loss Directions** | North | North | SE* | SW* | NE* | East |

**Note:** All directions afflicted in 2010 are marked with *. When a direction that is lucky for you is afflicted, you are recommended not to use that direction this year. When the direction afflicted is one of your bad luck directions, then you must extra sure you do not get hurt by facing this direction or occupying this location in your home or office.

vital to make sure that any lucky direction you may be facing - at work or at home which you had previously put into place - is not afflicted in 2010.

This is because time sensitive annual afflictions exert greater strength than personalized directions. Indeed annual energy flow usually possesses greater impact than Period energies. Time dimension feng shui affects the luck of the world more strongly than the space aspects of feng shui. Only when you practice your feng shui with this particular awareness, will you get the most out of it.

The table to the left summarizes the good and bad luck directions for Boar people.

## To Activate Success Luck

Your personalized success direction is your *sheng chi* direction. If you can face your success direction without being afflicted in any way by the annual afflictions then success luck flows smoothly, bringing advancement, growth and enhanced stature in your professional life. But you MUST make sure your success direction is not afflicted.

Look at your success direction for those born in the Boar year summarized in the table and you can systematically investigate which are the directions

## Success Luck for Boar People

| Kua Number | 1 | 4 | 7 | 2 | 5 | 8 |
|---|---|---|---|---|---|---|
| Male/Female | Female | Female | Female | Male | Male | Male |
| Success Direction | SE* | North | NW | NE* | NE* | SW* |

that are absolutely taboo for you. These mean your own bad luck directions as well as your good luck directions that are afflicted. Facing either of these directions will have an adverse effect on your success luck.

For 2010, the *sheng chi* direction of all Male Boars is afflicted by the illness or the *wu wang* stars which bring sickness and grave misfortunes; of the two, the SW *sheng chi* is the more badly affected. Thus for gentlemen Boars with Kua 8, and especially the **63 year old Fire Boar** and the **27 year old Water Boar,** it is better you give the SW a pass this year and face West instead. Note that West is very auspicious this year. West is flanked on both sides by the stars of Big Auspicious, and West is also your good relationship direction.

If you really have no choice and you cannot change your facing direction at work even when the direction is afflicted, then you should assess whether it is your success direction that is being hurt and if so, how strong the affliction is.

In this case, we have seen that the gentlemen Boars with their 2 or 8 Kua numbers have their success direction of NE afflicted!

So for all you Boar males, if you have no choice but to face your afflicted *sheng chi* directions, then those facing SW must place the **5 element pagoda** in front of them and wear the **5 element pagoda pendant**; while those facing the NE should use the **wu lou** symbol or the **Antahkarana** symbol.

As for Lady Boars, the **51 year old Earth lady Boar** and the **15 year old Wood teenager Boar** have their *sheng chi* direction of SE afflicted by the violent star 7. You should either avoid facing SE altogether in 2010, otherwise whatever success you achieve will be taken away from you; or you should place a **blue Rhino/ Elephant** in front of you on your desk, and also carry one with you at all times.

Those of you facing North will also be facing the Three Killings and this is fine, and is in fact very beneficial, except that it is a good idea to place the three celestial guardians on your desk as an additional safeguard. Directly confronting the Three Killings is one way to overcome its malicious energy.

The **63 and 39 year old Lady Boars** whose *sheng chi* is NW can face this NW direction without worrying about afflictions.

## Kua Number 1

From the chart, note that Lady Boars with Kua number 1 belong to the East group and for them their *sheng chi* success direction is afflicted by the violent burglary star. This indicates that if you face your success direction in 2010, the Year of the Tiger, your success will be robbed from under your nose.

There is betrayal and cheating going on that affect your chances of moving upward professionally. This year, you really must not allow other matters to distract you otherwise bad people who want what you have could succeed in politicking against you. The 51 year old Earth Boar lady as well as the 15 year old teenager girl, in particular must make sure not to face SE even though this is your *sheng chi*.

Note that Success luck in feng shui means that professional and working life going smoothly. When obstacles manifest, you can overcome them, and when troublesome people cause trouble for you, you can defeat them.

## Kua Number 4

From the chart, note that the lady Boar with Kua number 4 has North as their success direction. This brings literary success luck for the **39 year old Metal Boar lady**. This really brings excellent luck in 2010. It allows you to activate your *sheng chi* direction and also energizes it with water, as North is the place of water and Metal produces Water.

With the Three Killings direction there, directly staring down this affliction is an effective way of keeping this afflictive star under control. So facing North brings you success. But do remember to strenuously avoid sitting in or facing the NE and SW compass directions.

## Kua Number 7

The **63 year old Fire lady Boar,** as well as the **27 year old Water Boar lady** have Kua 7 so they belong to the West group. For you, your *sheng chi* success direction is NW which in 2010 is auspicious as it signifies future prosperity. There is a hidden threat of robbery afflicting this direction brought by the 24 Mountains Star but this is easily taken care of by placing a **blue**

**Rhino** here in the NW. Generally however, if you face the NW direction and you are also the main wage earner of the house, the direction is sure to serve you well this year.

Just to make sure you are not affected by those who might want to wish you harm, it is a good idea to keep the energy of your Five Ghost direction (i.e. South) strongly subdued. The South suffers from the quarrelsome star of 3 which brings heavy politicking and misunderstandings. Even when you walk away from trouble, others might find reason to stir up trouble against you. So simply avoiding facing the South is not enough, you must also place the remedy against the 3 star in the South.

Get the powerful **Magic Fire Wheel** to make sure no one with bad intentions can harm you. Note that the Fire Sword cure for the 3 star is not strong enough if this direction is also your 5 Ghosts direction, because the element of 5 Ghosts is also Fire. To overcome the five ghosts you need the magic fire wheel surrounded by a ring of fire! This is the correct symbol to overcome the 5 Ghosts (bad people) affliction as the wheel made of eight metal spokes is strong enough to keep

the 5 Ghosts properly subdued. This is even more important if you are in politics!

## Kua Number 2 & 5

All men born in a Boar year belong to the West group so they tend to benefit more from Period 8 than their female counterparts.

In 2010 however, Boar males have fewer opportunities as all three of their Kua numbers, 2, 5 and 8 seem to have afflicted directions as their *sheng chi*. The gentleman with Kua number 2 is the **75 year old Wood Boar** and the **39 year old Metal Boar**. The Boar with Kua 5 follows the lucky and unlucky directions of Kua 2 so NE is also its *sheng chi*.

However, the **51 year old Earth Boar** and the **15 year old Wood Boar** should note that since your Kua is 5, the Five Yellow is not necessarily your enemy. Indeed, those with Kua 5 usually enjoy indirect good fortune (usually brought by bad people) when the 5 flies into their location, so although you cannot face the NE, you can face the SW despite the 5 Yellow being there. You will not only be able to subdue this affliction, you might even benefit from it.

But in facing the NE, you can fall victim to the illness star. This means that if you use this direction as an aid to attracting success luck then whatever success comes your way comes at a cost to your health. Better to avoid this direction and let the year pass.

## Kua Number 8

The male Boar with Kua 8 is the **63 year old Fire Boar** and **26 year old Water Boar** who thus belong to the West group. For you, the SW direction is your success *sheng chi* direction and while this is simply excellent for the period of 8, in year 2010, the SW is afflicted by the *wu wang* which is a very serious and strong affliction.

The *wu wang* affliction will definitely cause you problems and it is better not to face the SW direction in 2010, as doing so brings a host of obstacles rather than success. It is better to face NW as this is the direction that has no negative connotations. You can also face West as this brings victory in competitive situations. The West is also very auspicious in 2010!

Meanwhile take note that your 5 Ghosts direction is North and unhappily for you the Three Killings affliction is also there in 2010. This direction is the source of people problems for you. Gossip and trouble making cause you some stress unless you ensure that the Three Killings are kept suppressed with the three celestials. Then also place the cure against the 5 Ghosts - the Magic Fire Wheel - here in the North. Finally, do make sure you do not face the North or sit in the North otherwise troublesome people are sure to cause you a lot of problems.

## To Maintain Good Health

These days, with international travel being so extensive and people around the world on the move so much, there is always the real danger of epidemics spreading across continents. Good health can no longer be taken for granted and it is now advisable not only to keep the energy of the home vibrant and clean, you must also make certain that where you live is always filled with a good supply of yang energy.

It is when chi energy is moving and not stagnating that residents within enjoy good health. A healthy home is where residents enjoy good resistance against bacteria and germs and are not in danger of picking up infectious disease. Thus good health in feng shui terms means you should eat well and auspiciously; and also live well with enough exercise and with no mental stress. When you have a good healthy environment, you are unlikely to be vulnerable to illness.

Sickness in any home is almost always due to bad feng shui and also because the house itself is affected by illness star vibrations which are left unchecked, or worse still, which flourish because the environment within fosters it. When someone gets sick in any household, the sickness energy is always infectious, so residents will get sick, one by one.

Apart from catching the bug from each other, this is also due to the illness star somehow getting activated; and then it affects everyone irrespective of which part of the house you stay in. Afflictive star influences can move from one part of the house to another if they are not strongly curbed **at source**. This means placing the **metal cures** and the **wu lou** in the **NE** corner which this year is the source of illness vibes.

**For those who want to capture your individual good health direction, you can sleep with the head pointed to your Health direction. This is said to be the direction of the "Heavenly Doctor".**

The table here shows the good health luck directions for all those born in the years of the Boar. Note that all male Boars have no problems with their health direction in 2010 and they can use their good health direction to recover from illness; but lady Boars with Kua numbers 4 and 7 have afflicted directions in 2010.

Those with Kua number 4 have South as their *tien yi* direction and in 2010, this has the quarrelsome 3 star which is bad for mental health, so it is advisable not to face South if you are ill.

## Health Directions for Boar

| Kua Number | 1 | 4 | 7 | 2 | 5 | 8 |
|---|---|---|---|---|---|---|
| Male/ Female | Female | Female | Female | Male | Male | Male |
| Health Direction | East | South* | SW* | West | West | NW |
| Bad Luck Direction | West | NW | North | East | East | South* |
| 6 Killings Direction | NW | West | SE* | South* | South* | East |

Those with Kua 7 have SW as their health direction and here the affliction is the *wu wang* which is also a very serious affliction, so the SW is best avoided.

## Becoming a Star at School

For the **15 year old Wood Boar** teenager, 2010 brings a good helping of success luck and even better health luck, so potential for you to emerge as a winner, a top student or excelling in the field of sports looks good.

The year also brings average confidence levels and self assurance, which is just enough to propel you towards getting the results for short and long term success. What you need to do to harness extra good luck is to make sure you sit facing your Personal Growth direction when you are studying at home, working on an assignment, doing your home work or sitting for an examination.

For the male, your best direction is NE, but unfortunately in 2010, the NE is afflicted by the illness star so the advice is for you to sit facing NW which will help you lay the groundwork for the future, and also the West which is very auspicious in 2010. Get yourself a a good compass and try to face either NW or West when you are studying or working.

For the female, the Personal Growth direction is the SE direction which is likewise afflicted in 2010 so this is not a good year to sit facing the SE. Here the violent star 7 is lurking around, bringing cheating luck, so sit facing North instead.

The North is Water which helps you benefit from this all-important element in 2010; but also because the North in 2010 houses the literary star, so this benefits those of you still at school. North is also your personal development direction, so for 2010, this is the direction for you!

# Attracting Romance

If you are looking for marriage opportunities, you must be careful that you do not meet up with married people pretending to be single. Be extra careful because the *flower of external romance* star is running amok in the Year of the Tiger.

This means the libido of married people, especially married men are at a high. Singles should thus be extra skeptical of new people coming into their lives, especially if they are actively using love rituals to attract romantic opportunities into their lives. Here are three ways to attract love:

1) First you can activate your personalized *peach blossom luck*. For the Boar, your peach blossom animal is the Rat. You should place a beautiful, expensive looking Rat in the North location of your bedroom. The Rat is considered as the creature that brings good income luck. The Rat is also known as being an excellent provider for the family, bringing sustenance and luck to its family, so do look for a beautiful Rat to attract a good romantic partner! Do not get a "Rat" from pavement stalls or flea markets where the energy they are absorbing is unlikely to be very good! Also make certain your Rat is not cracked or chipped!

2) The peach blossom star lands in the North in 2010. This is a powerful love direction for activating marriage luck. So no matter your age, irrespective of whether you have been married before, this is the direction to activate as well if you wish to benefit from the year's romantic energies.

3) Most effective of all is that you should sleep with your head pointed to your *nien yen* direction. This is shown below for the Boar men and women.

| Love Directions for Boar | | | | | | |
|---|---|---|---|---|---|---|
| **Kua Number** | 1 | 4 | 7 | 2 | 5 | 8 |
| **Male/ Female** | Female | Female | Female | Male | Male | Male |
| **Love Direction** | South* | East | NE* | NW | NW | West |

Sleeping with your head pointed to your love direction is the best way of attracting marriage luck for you; this will encourage *nien yen* vibrations to enter into your crown chakra while you sleep; but once again, do make certain that this direction is not afflicted during the year. The conventional advice to those wanting romance is for you to arrange your beds such that your head points to your *nien yen* direction when you sleep.

Based on this it appears that those of you lady Boars with Kua 1 and 7 have afflicted *nien yen* directions which are better not to activate. For the lady with East as her *nien yen,* this is a favorable direction in 2010.

Male Boars have no problems in their love lives this year and should they want to find love opportunities or if they are married and want children, then they should try to sleep with their heads pointed to their nien yen direction as shown. Both the NW and the West are auspicious directions.

## Interacting with the Annual Lo Shu Number 8

While the Feng Shui Chart reveals the energy pattern of the year, bringing new energies to every house, the new energies also interact with your personal Lo Shu charts. This is not to be confused with the Kua numbers discussed earlier. Every animal sign is influenced by three Lo Shu charts which are created using their birth Lo Shu numbers. These numbers apply to both men and women. The table on the next page reveals the Lo Shu number of those born in the years of the Boar extracted from the Thousand Year calendar. Take note that the Boar's Lo

Shu numbers are 2, 8 or 5 which reflects a number from each Lower, Middle and Upper period in the feng shui cycle of 3 periods which covers 180 years. The Lo Shu number at birth offers clues to the personality traits of the Boar and how the number interacts with the current year's Lo Shu number offer clues and recommendations to improve the year's feng shui luck for the Boar.

## Lo Shu Numbers of Boar

| Birth Year | Element Boar | Age in 2010 | Lo Shu No. at Birth |
|---|---|---|---|
| 1935 | Wood Boar | 75 | 2 |
| 1947 | Fire Boar | 63 | 8 |
| 1959 | Earth Boar | 51 | 5 |
| 1971 | Metal Boar | 39 | 2 |
| 1983 | Water Boar | 27 | 8 |
| 1995 | Wood Boar | 15 | 5 |

# Boar with Birth Lo Shu of 2
(affecting the 75 & 39 year old Boars)

| SE | S | SW |
|:---:|:---:|:---:|
| 1 | 6 | 8 |
| 9 (E) | **2** | 4 (W) |
| 5 | 7 | 3 |
| NE | N | NW |

This is the Lo Shu chart for the 75 & 39 year old Boars.

Boars born under the Lo Shu number of 2 are extremely charming people. You have a way with words that make you enticing and persuasive. Your life improves as you get older but in your early years you may not feel close to your parents.

The number 2 is enhanced by the number 8 as together they make up the sum of ten - an auspicious combination which attracts a special kind of good fortune. Take good care of your health in 2010. It is beneficial to make a donation to an old folks home or to a hospital, or any kind of charity as this will help you cross into good health.

# Boar with Birth Lo Shu of 8
(affecting the 63 and 27 year old Boars)

| SE | S | SW |
|:---:|:---:|:---:|
| 7 | 3 | 5 |
| 6 | **8** | 1 |
| 2 | 4 | 9 |
| NE | N | NW |

E — W

This is the Lo Shu chart for the 63 & 27 year old Boars.

The number 8 is the luckiest number of the current Period of 8 and is also the strongest. It stands for current prosperity and when considered in the light of this year's Lo Shu number of 8 we see its strength seriously strengthened. This means that those of you born in the years with Lo shu 8 will enjoy excellent opportunities in 2010.

Boars born under the Lo Shu of 8 are usually kind hearted and soft inside so you are someone with a heart of gold. You are also witty and endowed with excellent memory power. If you have a mole or some kind of birthmark on the right side of your cheek, your hip or your leg, you are destined to have a very easy going life. In 2010, you must light up the center of your home enhancing fire energy here; and in your North or at the entrance of your hose activate with a water feature. Using these enhancers will bring exceptional opportunities for you!

## Boar with Birth Lo Shu of 5
(affecting the 51 and 15 year old Boar)

| SE | S | SW |
|:--:|:-:|:--:|
| 4 | 9 | 2 |
| 3 | 5 | 7 |
| 8 | 1 | 6 |
| NE | N | NW |

This is the Lo Shu chart for the 51 & 15 year old Boars.

The number 5 is a very special number in Chinese Astrology as it is the number that bridges the low numbers with the high. The number 5 is also the center number of the original Lo Shu grid. Boars born with this Lo Shu number have a store of knowledge and are described as being "rich with wisdom". They are very spiritual possessing strong faith in their religion. They are smart, quick thinking and witty. For male Boars, they are also influenced by the Lo shu number of 2 while female Boars are influenced by the number 8. In 2010, the number 5 belongs to the trinity of Earth with the year's number 8, so you can also indirectly benefit from the number 8. Activate the centre of the home with Fire and the entrance in to the home with Water. This will improve your luck considerably.

## Safeguarding Boar's Location in 2010

Use a compass to determine the Boar direction of your home which is NW3. This refers to the NW sector of the whole house and the NW corner of rooms you frequently use, such as your bedroom or your home office.

You should make sure the toilet, storeroom and kitchen are NOT located in the NW. If they are, it will create a serious feng shui problem for you. A **toilet** in your Boar direction flushes away all the luck of residents belonging to the Boar sign. Career luck is hard hit and recognition will be blocked. Those in business face an array of problems including financial loss. A **store room** here locks up all your good luck. You will find it hard to fly and ambitions will get stalled. A **kitchen** here suppresses all your good luck. If you envisage staying in the same home for several more years, and there is a toilet or store room here in your home location, you should change the room usage of your NW sector.

When you create an active space where your productive work gets done, it energizes your most personally important sector of the home. This benefits you. Always make sure the energy here is vibrant and active, yang in nature and never has a chance to get stale allowing yin chi to accumulate. Changing the usage of the room can be beneficial.

## Improving your Door Feng Shui

One of the best ways of improving your feng shui in any year is to ensure that the doors you use daily into the house, into your bedroom and into your office are auspicious for you. To determine the best direction to use we always look at the four auspicious directions using the Kua formula of directions. You can check the tables in this book for all your lucky directions but what we have done is to summarize the best door facing directions for you based on your *sheng chi* direction and also we have given you our advice on best directions for each of you in 2010. We are suggesting alternatives for those whose *sheng chi* are afflicted.

## Auspicious Door Directions for Boar

| Kua Number | 1 | 4 | 7 | 2 | 5 | 8 |
|---|---|---|---|---|---|---|
| Male/Female | Female | Female | Female | Male | Male | Male |
| Best Door Direction based on Sheng Chi Direction | SE | North | NW | NE | NE | SW |
| Best Door Facing Direction in 2010 | North | North | NW | NW | NW | West |

Use a compass to determine the facing direction that works best for you, and try to use only doors that are lucky for you in any year. Be mindful about the doors you walk under each day and update this every year. This means checking for afflictions to your doors. For 2010, all doors that either face, or are located in the SW, NE, South, North and SE are afflicted and will respond positively to antidote remedies.

Here is the list of remedies you can place either above the door, or flanking it. The more frequently you use the door, the more important it is to place these remedies. Doors referred to also include doors inside the home. These remedies do not send out harmful chi the way the Pa Kua symbol with yin arrangement of trigrams do. In the past, these were the only "cure" known and sold, and many used them indiscriminately without realizing the potential harm they can cause. The remedies recommended here can easily correct and subdue afflictions without creating bad chi. This is a very important aspect of cures that we take seriously into consideration.

For all **main doors** going into the home, it is an excellent idea also to place **powerful mantra plaques** done in red and this is because the mantras not only keep all bad vibes out of the house, they also bless everyone who walks under them. This is the best way to practice feng shui – to make sure it benefits you without harming others!

- **For doors facing Southwest,** place the **five element plaque** above the door.
- **For doors facing Northeast,** place the **wu lou door hanging** by the side of the door.
- **For doors facing South,** place the **kalachakra mantra plaque** above the door.
- **For doors facing North,** place the **three celestial guardians** flanking the door.
- **For doors facing Southeast,** place **blue Rhino/Elephant door hangings** flanking the door.

Use a good reliable compass to determine your facing direction of all your doors and make sure you stand just in front of the door to determine this. Do note that even when the "door" you use to enter the house is from the garage, and it is only a small side door, it is still very important. In fact, the more you use a door, the more important it becomes.

## Special Enhancers & Amulets for 2010

To ensure stability of luck for your household, it is an excellent idea to activate the center of the home, or at least the center of your living room area with a **crystal globe containing blue colored water**. We have designed a very special globe in two sizes - a 3 inch diameter globe and a 6 inch diameter globe that is embossed on the outside with the 12 animal signs of the Zodiac. The globe is an excellent enhancer for the center number of 8 because this is an Earth number. The Earth element also signifies wealth luck in 2010 so the presence of a crystal globe here is very auspicious. It is beneficial to twirl the globe daily to imbue it with yang energy.

The water inside symbolically brings much needed Water element into the living area. This is because the paht chee chart tells us that Water is terribly lacking in 2010. Note that to Taoist masters, even "a single drop of water can represent an entire ocean". Hence water enhancers are so good for 2010!

For the Boar person, it is an excellent idea to place the Boar image next to the globe, letting it face NW. This creates good energy for your particular animal sign and should you so wish, you can also place your secret friend the Tiger, as well as your allies, the Rabbit and Sheep images here as well. This will create excellent friendship energy bringing harmony and balance into your life. Special note for Boar -note your ally the Horse enjoys good luck this year, so stick close to this ally!

## Special Talismans for the Boar

In 2010, the Boar person benefits from the following cures and talismans:

Vairocana plaque

- The **Vairocana Plaque** to protect you from any harmed by weapons, fire, water, poisons, black magic and natural disaster. This plaque contains the heart mantra of the Buddha Vairocana. Display it in your animal sign direction of NW to help you overcome the Robbery Star from the 24 Mountains.

- Carry the **Blue Rhino and Elephant** to counter robbery threats from the 24 Mountains in your chart this year. Lady Boars should also carry the **Night Spot Protection Amulet** if they are out alone at night a lot.

Blue Rhino and Elephant keychain.

- Carry the **Wealth Crane Talisman** to bring you promotion luck this year. The wealth crane is the highest ranked bird in the Emperor courthouse. Featured on the back of this amulet is the wealth vase to ensure your promotion in rank comes with a promotion in salary.

- A **Metal Wu Lou** to subdue the illness star of 2010. This is particularly important for the Boar in the months of March, September and January 2011.

- Wear some **Om Mani jewellery** in gold. Wearing protective mantras against your body will help protect you from all kinds of harm. It will also attract good fortune luck to you in a year when your Horoscope Luck Elements look good when combined with the year's elements.

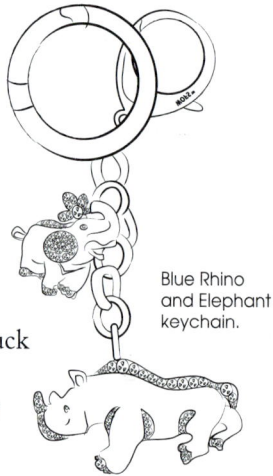

- Display the **9 Ring Sword** in the NW of your home and office. This power sword helps to enhance the number 9 in your home location of NW as well as control the robbery afflictions in your chart. This sword is also an enhancer for a good reputation, fame and recognition luck.

- Hang the **Tai Sui Plaque** in the NE sector to appease the Grand Duke Jupiter and to bring good luck. This plaque has been designed with Tai Sui at the top, with the Pi Yao talisman at the bottom to overcome the Tai Sui. This plaque brings good energy to the home and will also protect againt intruders and people with bad intentions entering your home.

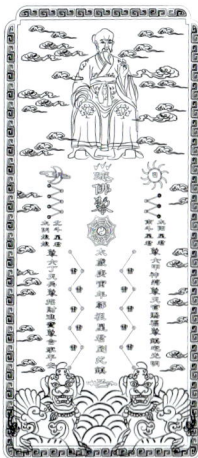

Tai Sui plaque

# The 24 Mountains in 2010

The number 8 dominates the year 2010 bringing auspicious energy to the Tiger Year. The 12 animals signs play host to the stars of the 24 mountains. These indicate the kind of cosmic forces influencing the luck for the year.

# WANT TO LEARN MORE?

## Don't Stop Now!

We hope you enjoyed reading your own personal horoscope book from Lillian Too & Jennifer Too. You are probably already feeling a difference in your life and enjoying the results of actions you have taken!

## So, What's Next?

## LILLIAN TOO'S FREE
### Online Weekly Ezine NEW!

It's FREE! The latest weekly news and Feng Shui updates from Lillian herself! Learn more of her secrets and open your mind to deeper feng shui today.

Just go online to www.lilliantoomandalaezine.com and sign up today!

## LILLIAN TOO's FREE NEW
### Online Weekly Ezine!

**Don't Miss Out!** Join thousands of others who are already receiving their **FREE** updates delivered to their inbox each week.

**Lillian's NEW Online FREE Weekly Ezine is only available to those who register online at www.lilliantoomandalaezine.com**